HOMELAND SECURITY
OPERATIONAL ANALYSIS CENTER

The Cost of Cost-Effectiveness

Expanding Equity in Federal Emergency Management Agency Hazard Mitigation Assistance Grants

BENJAMIN M. MILLER, NOREEN CLANCY, DOUGLAS C. LIGOR, GEOFFREY KIRKWOOD, DAVID METZ, STEVEN KOLLER, STEPHANIE STEWART

This research was published in 2023.

About This Report

The Federal Emergency Management Agency (FEMA) operates multiple hazard mitigation assistance (HMA) grant programs as a way to promote a national culture of preparedness and public safety, mitigate the consequences that disasters have for communities and infrastructure, and reduce future draws on the Disaster Relief Fund. The Robert T. Stafford Disaster Relief and Emergency Assistance Act (Pub. L. 93-288, 1974, as amended and codified at U.S. Code, Title 42, Chapter 68) requires FEMA to ensure that these mitigation activities are cost-effective. To determine cost-effectiveness, FEMA currently requires any project seeking an HMA grant to include a benefit–cost analysis (BCA), implemented in accordance with Office of Management and Budget Circular A-94. Applicants and subapplicants of mitigation grants have provided extensive feedback that the BCA process is cumbersome and that finding the right data to include in the calculations of costs and benefits is difficult. FEMA is concerned that the administrative burdens and the costs of application processes could discourage subapplicants with fewer resources from applying or place them at a disadvantage in developing quality applications. Furthermore, two 2021 executive orders direct federal agencies to achieve greater equity and fairness in allocating federal resources. Two HMA grant programs have been selected as pilot programs for the corresponding federalwide Justice40 Initiative.

It is within this context that FEMA engaged the Homeland Security Operational Analysis Center (HSOAC), a federally funded research and development center (FFRDC) operated by the RAND Corporation for the U.S. Department of Homeland Security (DHS), to explore how the BCA process could be simplified to be more inclusive of lower-resourced communities. The analysis and conclusions in this report are those of the authors and not FEMA. FEMA is under no obligation to accept findings or implement options presented here.

This research was sponsored by FEMA and conducted in the Disaster Management and Resilience Program of RAND's Homeland Security Research Division, which operates HSOAC.

About the Homeland Security Operational Analysis Center

The Homeland Security Act of 2002 (Section 305 of Public Law 107-296, as codified at U.S. Code, Title 6, Section 185) authorizes the Secretary of Homeland Security, acting through the Under Secretary for Science and Technology, to establish one or more FFRDCs to provide independent analysis of homeland security issues. The RAND Corporation operates HSOAC as an FFRDC for DHS under contract HSHQDC-16-D-00007.

The HSOAC FFRDC provides the government with independent and objective analyses and advice in core areas important to the department in support of policy development, decisionmaking, alternative approaches, and new ideas on issues of significance. The HSOAC FFRDC also works with and supports other federal, state, local, tribal, and public- and private-sector organizations that make up the homeland security enterprise. The HSOAC FFRDC's research is undertaken by mutual consent with DHS and is organized as a set of discrete tasks. This report presents the results of research and analysis conducted under task order 70FA6021F00000016, "Proposed Approach for a Review of FEMA's Cost Effectiveness Assessments."

The results presented in this report do not necessarily reflect official DHS opinion or policy.

For more information on the Homeland Security Research Division, see www.rand.org/hsrd. For more information on this publication, see www.rand.org/t/RRA2171-1.

Acknowledgments

We are grateful to staff within FEMA and the BCA team within the Data Analytics Section who supplied information, data, and insights necessary to conduct this research. We also sincerely thank interviewees from within FEMA and other federal entities, including the U.S. Army Corps of Engineers, the U.S. Department of Housing and Urban Development, the U.S. Department of Transportation, and the Federal Aviation Administration, who shared their experiences and perspectives with us. We are also extremely appreciative of support from Gabriel Leonard, a quantitative research assistant at RAND. Finally, we are grateful for the impressively insightful comments provided by the reviewers of this study: Craig A. Bond, senior economist at RAND, and Scott Davis, urban planner and principal of SGD Urban Solutions.

Summary

Issue

The Federal Emergency Management Agency (FEMA) operates multiple hazard mitigation assistance (HMA) grant programs as a way to promote a national culture of preparedness and public safety, mitigate the consequences that disasters have for communities and infrastructure, and reduce future draws on the Disaster Relief Fund. The three programs falling into the broad category of HMA are the Hazard Mitigation Grant Program (HMGP), Flood Mitigation Assistance (FMA) program, and Building Resilient Infrastructure and Communities (BRIC) program.

The Stafford Act requires FEMA to ensure that mitigation activities supported with HMA program funds are cost-effective. For an HMA-funded project to be considered cost-effective, it must have a benefit–cost ratio (BCR) that is greater than or equal to 1, indicating that the present value of project benefits exceeds costs. To determine cost-effectiveness, FEMA currently requires any project seeking HMA grants to include a benefit–cost analysis (BCA), implemented in accordance with Office of Management and Budget (OMB) Circular A-94. Applicants and subapplicants to the HMA grant programs have provided extensive feedback that the BCA process is cumbersome and that finding the right data to include in the calculations of costs and benefits is difficult. FEMA is concerned that the administrative burdens and the costs of its application processes could discourage subapplicants with fewer resources from applying or place them at a disadvantage in developing quality applications. Research has demonstrated that FEMA disaster response funding, as well as mitigation grant programs, are perpetuating inequities by funding more efforts in wealthier, whiter communities. Furthermore, two 2021 executive orders (EOs), EO 13985 and EO 14008, direct federal agencies to achieve greater equity and fairness in allocating federal resources. Two of the HMA grant programs have been selected as pilot programs for the corresponding federalwide Justice40 Initiative.

It is within this context that FEMA asked the Homeland Security Operational Analysis Center (HSOAC) to explore how the BCA process could be simplified to be more inclusive of lower-resourced communities.

Approach

To undertake this study, the HSOAC team began by reviewing FEMA's current BCA methodology (Chapter 2). We then reviewed the literature documenting equity challenges the current approach presents to subapplicants, potential alternatives or changes to the BCA process, and relevant insights from HMA program data (Chapter 3). We then reviewed the authorities that dictate how the BCA process must function, as represented by the legal, regulatory, and policy frameworks under which the grant programs are administered (Chapter 4). Finally, we spoke with officials from other federal entities that use BCA processes in administering nonregulatory grant programs, and benchmarked the requirements and methodologies of those grant programs relative to those of FEMA's grant programs (Chapter 5).

Key Findings

The findings from these analyses identify potential alternative approaches that might be relevant for FEMA's efforts to improve equity of access to HMA grants while still meeting legal and regulatory requirements (see Chapter 6). This section summarizes some of the key findings from each aspect of our analysis.

FEMA's Dual Goals of Equity and Simplicity Occasionally Compete

FEMA administers multiple grant programs that fall into the category of HMA or HMA programs. These are HMGP, the FMA program, and BRIC. Subapplications for competitive BRIC and FMA funding exceeded available funds by factors of four and three, respectively, in fiscal year (FY) 2021, and the amount of available funds was increased substantially for FY 2022. Despite this popularity, some applicants and subapplicants regard the BCA component of the application process as cumbersome and a barrier to applying for funding. These concerns remain despite FEMA's efforts to ease the burden of conducting BCA to meet HMA programs' cost-effectiveness requirements, such as development of the publicly available BCA Toolkit. FEMA is concerned that the administrative burdens and the costs of its application processes could discourage subapplicants with fewer resources from applying or place them at a disadvantage in developing quality applications.

The communities that develop and intend to carry out mitigation projects are often referred to as *subapplicants* because these communities must apply through designated applicants, which are typically states, territories, or federally recognized tribes (FEMA, 2015). An applicant submits one application to FEMA that may consist of multiple subapplications, typically representing requests by individual communities. Because competition essentially occurs at the applicant level and not the national level, applicants have substantial influence over which subapplicants ultimately receive HMA funding. FEMA has little control over applicants' processes for determining which subapplications are sent to FEMA. However, concerns have been raised about potential inequities in FEMA's distribution of HMA funds. For example, a handful of states on the east and west coasts are slated to receive 90 percent of all FY 2020 BRIC funds (FEMA, 2021g; Headwaters Economics, 2021a). Research has demonstrated that FEMA disaster response funding, as well as mitigation grant programs, are perpetuating inequities by funding more efforts in wealthier, whiter communities (Elliott, Brown, and Loughran, 2020; Frank, 2022; Howell and Elliott, 2019; Mach et al., 2019).

FEMA and, in turn, we are pursuing dual and occasionally competing objectives of (1) achieving a more equitable distribution of HMA funds and (2) simplifying the application process. As discussed in this report and in Finucane et al. (forthcoming), achieving a more equitable distribution of HMA funds might require more-precise specification of beneficiaries and associated equity metrics. Depending on the nature of any changes to HMA processes, efforts to collect such information could increase, rather than decrease, application complexity. Furthermore, some simplifications to HMA processes might reduce burdens for all applicants and thus might not directly address inequities in the distribution of HMA funds.

It is reasonable to consider whether simplification of the BCA process is an appropriate goal. Simplification could result in a less accurate quantification of benefits, thereby reducing FEMA's ability to award funds to the projects for which the net benefits would be greatest. However, FEMA's current process for selecting which projects to fund is not necessarily designed to select projects with the highest BCRs. The role of BCA in FEMA's current processes is more accurately described as a cost-effectiveness threshold for determining eligibility than as an award process based on BCA. Almost every project must have a BCR that is greater than or equal to 1 to be eligible for HMA funds (notable exceptions being HMGP's 5 Percent Initiative and projects that use ecosystem service benefits). However, subapplications with higher BCRs do not receive any advantage over applications with lower eligible BCRs. As a result, interviews and data suggest that many BRIC subapplicants tend to submit BCAs with BCRs slightly above 1, likely because of program requirements for projects to be cost-effective rather than maximize net benefits. Instead, projects are ranked based on points that are awarded for meeting different criteria, such as being an infrastructure project, incorporating nature-based solutions, and the community's Building Code Effectiveness Grading Schedule rating (a measure of a community's building codes and building code enforcement).

In FY 2022, FEMA updated its requirements for BRIC and FMA grants in an effort to more directly consider equity and distributional factors. It uses the Centers for Disease Control and Prevention's Social

Vulnerability Index (SVI) as a tool to identify disadvantaged areas. Specifically, if a subapplicant has an SVI score greater than or equal to 0.8 and is "competitive and otherwise eligible" but is unable to calculate a BCA, "FEMA may assist such communities with developing a BCA" (Hazard Mitigation Assistance Division, 2022). As discussed in Chapter 3, FEMA's assistance in navigating the BCA process might help lower-resourced communities successfully document their projects' cost-effectiveness, which could push them into eligibility. Chapter 3 also discusses how FEMA has incorporated distributional considerations into the process of selecting which eligible projects receive funding, although this selection process is separate and subsequent to the use of BCA to determine eligibility based on cost-effectiveness. Although a BCA might note or describe the people or communities that will face costs or benefit from the project, such distributional concerns do not traditionally affect BCR calculations and therefore do not affect BCR-based eligibility determinations.

FEMA Has the Authority to Implement Recommended Changes

With FEMA's desire to make adjustments to its current mitigation grant funding process to integrate issues of equity, it needed to understand its legal guardrails. A key task for the HSOAC team was to examine the legal, regulatory, and policy frameworks under which the grant programs are administered and thereby assess the extent to which these authorities permit or limit changes to FEMA's existing BCA processes. We employed a five-step methodological process, described in Chapter 4, to examine and assess authorities' role and impact on FEMA's administration of the mitigation grant process. In sum, we found that the authorities applicable to the mitigation grant programs provide FEMA the ability to change, amend, or revise its current policies, processes, and procedures in a manner that the agency determines facilitates greater equitable access and delivery of grants. This finding is important because FEMA personnel told us in interviews that FEMA has been deferring such decisions to OMB.

FEMA's statutory authority for conducting HMA programs is found within the Stafford Act, the landmark legislation passed in 1988 governing federal disaster response and recovery activities. Under the Stafford Act, FEMA HMA programs are required only to be cost-effective, a requirement that is repeated in the statutory language authorizing these programs. We found that FEMA is the federal agency authorized to interpret the meaning of the term *cost-effective* because that term is referenced in the Stafford Act and its implementing regulations at Title 44 of the Code of Federal Regulations (C.F.R.). FEMA may apply either a cost-effectiveness analysis or a BCA to evaluate HMA grant applications so long as the selected method complies with a reasonable interpretation of the term *cost-effective* as that term is referenced in the Stafford Act and its implementing regulations at Title 44 of the C.F.R.

Furthermore, we found that FEMA is the federal agency authorized to interpret and apply the guidance contained in OMB Circular A-94. FEMA is not bound by guidance contained in OMB Circular A-94 if the agency determines that the guidance conflicts or is otherwise inconsistent with the Stafford Act, its implementing regulations at Title 44 of the C.F.R., or any EOs that FEMA is charged to administer. For example, FEMA may apply a discount rate for the evaluation of HMA grant applications based on the U.S. Treasury borrowing rate, a 7-percent discount rate, or any rate in between based on criteria that the agency reasonably determines.

FEMA's Approach to BCA Differs from Those of Other Federal Entities

FEMA is not the only federal agency that uses BCA to guide federal grant allocations. Although aspects of BCA methodologies are similar across federal agencies, FEMA's BCA methodology differed from other federal agencies' methodologies in several ways.

First, most agencies require only projects that exceed a certain cost threshold to conduct a formal BCA. This might reduce concerns about administrative cost barriers for applications from smaller disadvantaged communities.

Second, other agencies consider a wider variety of potential benefits in the BCA—including nonmonetized benefits (e.g., social cohesion, quality-of-life improvements)—which might help an applicant with hard-to-quantify benefits achieve a higher BCR to meet the minimum evaluation criterion. Most agencies, including FEMA, expressed interest in considering as wide a variety of benefits as possible. In some cases, officials reported viewing particular categories of benefits as not relevant to their program's objectives or expressed the need for caution to avoid erroneously categorizing transfers as benefits.

Third, although other agencies generally follow OMB's directive to use a 7-percent discount rate as the base-case analysis, some agencies allow applicants to also present alternative analyses using different discount rates, so long as that different (typically lower) rate is justified. This could improve the attractiveness of the BCR calculation for projects with long-term benefits, particularly environmental or social benefits, and ensure that those types of projects are not unduly disqualified. However, this view was not uniform: Others said that Circular A-94 clearly prescribed the use of a 7-percent discount rate with little room for alternative interpretations.

Fourth, in most programs, the BCR factors directly into award selection criteria along with other factors. This provides an opportunity to appropriately weight nonmonetized benefits in the evaluation process to address equity considerations, rather than automatically disqualifying any project that does not have a BCR greater than 1.

Possible Changes to FEMA's BCA Process

Our findings helped us identify nine changes that FEMA could implement to address inequities introduced by the use of BCA in the HMA grant process. These options are not mutually exclusive; FEMA could elect to implement some combination of these options. In some cases, implementing one option would alter the ways in which another option might be implemented. This report focuses on the identification of options and does not provide potential implementation approaches.

Option 1: Replace the BCA with a Simpler Measure of Cost-Effectiveness

FEMA has historically chosen to use BCA to establish cost-effectiveness, but FEMA has the authority to issue new policy guidance to change the methodology used to establish cost-effectiveness.

Option 2: Establish a Minimum Cost Threshold or Other Criteria for a Full BCA

FEMA could establish a cost threshold below which a project would not be required to complete a full BCA to demonstrate cost-effectiveness. This could reduce the burden of preparing a subapplication for small projects, for which requiring a BCA could easily cause an otherwise cost-effective project to no longer be cost-effective and thus remove a factor that could be discouraging communities with limited resources from submitting subapplications.

Option 3: Allow Applicants to Include Alternative Discount Rates

FEMA has the legal authority to provide alternative guidance on interest rates if desired; neither the legal authorities identified in this report nor OMB Circular A-94 prescribes that FEMA must use a 7-percent discount rate when evaluating the future value presented by grant applicants. The ideal discount rate would accurately reflect the present value of future costs and benefits to the applicant, plus a premium that reflects the risk of project benefits not accruing. Unfortunately, it is not possible to precisely quantify this theoretically ideal discount rate, which likely varies across time, communities, and projects. The most practical approach might be to consider multiple interest rates to illustrate the extent to which the choice of interest rate influences cost-effectiveness.

Option 4: Consider Broader Types of Benefits

The benefits allowed by different federal discretionary grant programs, as well as infrastructure planning, vary significantly. FEMA could consider expanding the types of benefits allowable within HMA programs' subapplication evaluation criteria, especially those unquantified or excluded benefits that might accrue to disadvantaged communities but are not captured in current BCAs. Examples include projects' impacts on residents' quality of life, environmental and ecological factors, and operational cost savings.

Option 5: Apply Distributional Weights to Benefit and Cost Calculations

Using a distributional weighting scheme to weight benefits and costs according to some indicator of beneficiary welfare (e.g., income) might allow for a distribution of program benefits that more equitably considers distributional concerns.

Option 6: Incorporate BCA and Ratios More Clearly into the Award Decision

FEMA could incorporate the BCR or other aspects of the BCA more fully into the evaluation process, beyond solely serving as an eligibility criterion. This change would not address FEMA's concerns about complexity but would incentivize subapplicants to more fully account for project benefits, which might be important for FEMA to see that 40 percent of program benefits would flow to disadvantaged communities in accordance with Justice40 goals.

Option 7: Change FEMA Large Project Notification Reporting Practices

Consolidated Appropriations Act, 2022 (Pub. L. 117-103), requires FEMA to notify Congress of awards greater than $1 million no later than three business days prior to obligating the grant or project funds. FEMA currently submits projects above the large project notification threshold to OMB for review prior to submitting to Congress or even Department of Homeland Security leadership, although doing so is not required. This relationship with OMB differs from OMB's relationships with other federal agencies. If it so chooses, FEMA could discontinue providing large project notification to OMB; our interpretation is that there is no legal requirement for substantive review or its concurrence, approval, or denial of HMA project-level applications. By ending this practice, FEMA might save staff time and expedite obligation of HMA program funds to recipients.

Option 8: Precisely Specify Benefiting Areas

Determining which communities benefit from a given HMA-funded project is crucial for achieving equity objectives. Yet HMA programs have not historically collected precise or standardized information about a project's benefiting area (that is, the area that the project would benefit). By collecting more-precise information about projects' benefiting areas in subapplications, FEMA can better ensure that program benefits flow as intended with regard to objectives, such as the Justice40 goal of delivering 40 percent of benefits to disadvantaged communities.

Option 9: Encourage Applicants to Solicit Subapplications from Disadvantaged Communities

Once FEMA has developed a durable metric with which to measure and assign disadvantaged community status to communities applying for HMA program funds, FEMA might more proactively and strategically encourage new subapplications from qualifying communities that have not previously participated in HMA programs. Given the level of discretion and influence that applicants (typically, states, territories, or federally recognized tribes) have in the HMA process, FEMA should engage not only with disadvantaged communities but also with the HMA applicants.

Contents

Figures and Tables

Figures

Tables

Introduction

The frequency and severity of natural disasters are increasing over time partly because of climate change and the increased concentration of people and assets in areas exposed to those natural hazards (Hayhoe et al., 2018). From 1980 to 2021 in the United States, an annual average of 7.7 natural disasters each caused more than $1 billion in damage, with an average cost of $52.4 billion per event (consumer price index adjusted). However, in the past five years (2017 to 2021), the annual average was 17.8 natural disasters that resulted in more than $1 billion in damage, with an average cost of $152.9 billion per event (consumer price index adjusted) (National Centers for Environmental Information, undated). Overall, the number of billion-dollar disasters has more than doubled, and the cost per disaster has nearly tripled. Communities struggle to contend with the increasing frequency and associated costs of natural disasters.

The mission of the Federal Emergency Management Agency (FEMA) is to help people before, during, and after disasters. One way in which FEMA approaches this mission is through hazard mitigation assistance (HMA) grants, which provide funding to state, local, territorial, and tribal governments for eligible mitigation actions. This funding is intended to promote a national culture of preparedness and public safety and to spur investments that mitigate the consequences that disasters have for communities and infrastructure. Investments in mitigation improve overall community resilience, reduce the country's overall risk portfolio, and reduce future draws on the Disaster Relief Fund (DRF).

Legal, regulatory, and policy requirements govern how FEMA can distribute HMA funds. First and foremost, the Robert T. Stafford Disaster Relief and Emergency Assistance Act (Pub. L. 93-288, 1974, as amended and codified at U.S. Code, Title 42, Chapter 68) requires FEMA to ensure that mitigation activities funded by HMA grants are cost-effective. Cost-effectiveness has historically been solidly achieved; independent estimates of the average savings due to such federal predisaster mitigation (PDM) programs range from $4 to $6 of averted losses per $1 spent (Godschalk et al., 2009; Multi-Hazard Mitigation Council, 2019). As a matter of policy, FEMA uses benefit–cost analysis (BCA) to determine whether proposed mitigation activities are cost-effective and defines a project as cost-effective if it has a benefit–cost ratio (BCR) of 1 or greater. FEMA instructs applicants (and subapplicants) to submit BCAs that follow guidance from the Office of Management and Budget's (OMB's) Circular A-94.

However, there are concerns about FEMA's current process for determining cost-effectiveness. Applicants (and subapplicants) report that completing the BCA portion of the grant application requires an inordinate amount of resources and data (FEMA, 2020a; GAO, 2021). Completing a BCA often requires hiring contractors to assist with the process, which might discourage low-resourced communities from applying. As a result, applicants and subapplicants have expressed "consistent dissatisfaction with perceived biases and lack of flexibility in the BCA methodology" (FEMA, 2020a, p. iv).

FEMA, along with most other federal agencies, measures the impact of natural disasters primarily by the monetary value of damage to physical assets or avoided losses to those assets. There are concerns that benefits and costs are too narrowly defined and that only benefits that can be monetized can be included in the BCA. Other concerns relate to the focus on the costs and benefits to physical assets within the BCA that puts lower-resourced and rural communities at a disadvantage (Frank, 2021; Headwater Economics, 2021b; Junod et al.,

2021). Rural communities also lack the density of structures needed to reach sufficiently high benefit values. These conditions put lower-resourced and rural communities at a disadvantage relative to wealthier, urban communities in terms of successfully reaching a BCR of 1 or greater.

Both empirical research and investigative analysis have demonstrated that FEMA disaster response funding and mitigation grant program funding are perpetuating inequities by funding more efforts in wealthier, whiter communities (Elliott, Brown, and Loughran, 2020; Frank, 2022; Howell and Elliott, 2019; Mach et al., 2019). These inequities have been attributed in large part to the BCA process. FEMA staff who review the subapplications have observed that mitigation projects that include lower-resourced communities might be likelier to try to meet the BCR threshold by relying on other types of benefits, including broader social impacts, such as public health, social cohesion (e.g., avoiding displacement of some residents), or improved recreation. These benefits are often more challenging to quantify than benefits to physical aspects.

For these reasons, FEMA is under pressure from applicants and subapplicants to simplify the BCA process and make it more equitable. All applicants, not just disadvantaged communities, can benefit from a simpler application process. FEMA has proposed various adjustments to the BCA method and process in an attempt to lighten the burden on communities, such as requiring a BCA only for projects over a certain dollar value. However, OMB has also recommended that FEMA develop a more mathematically robust process to justify cost-effectiveness, and such a process might require applicants and subapplicants to provide additional data. The rationale for requesting a more mathematically robust process is not clear because there is strong evidence that most federal PDM projects are cost-effective, as noted earlier (Godschalk et al., 2009; Multi-Hazard Mitigation Council, 2019). Furthermore, any changes to the application process must be in keeping with legal and regulatory requirements and the overall mission of the HMA grant programs.

To help resolve these competing interests, FEMA engaged the Homeland Security Operational Analysis Center (HSOAC), a federally funded research and development center operated by the RAND Corporation for the U.S. Department of Homeland Security (DHS), to review the legal, regulatory, policy, and methodological framework of current BCA processes to consider whether changes in interpretation or methodological approach might be appropriate.

Policy Context

Although FEMA's BCA process has evolved over many years, there is a continued need to reexamine its approach to ensure that resources are equitably and expansively matched to potential applicants. FEMA is open to considering a wide variety of potential changes that might help address these issues, such as simplifying the BCA process or broadening benefits to include more social benefits and expanding when those can be applied. FEMA has implemented recent changes meant to simplify the BCA process, including the following:

- revisions to the BCA software that significantly reduced the data inputs required and improved the user interface
- policy adjustments that allow project BCAs to count ancillary benefits of projects—such as ecosystem service benefits—regardless of the BCR from risk reduction benefits
- creation of a set of precalculated benefits[1] that applicants and subapplicants can use as part of their BCA calculations. The applicants and subapplicants have reported finding these useful, and some have requested more precalculated benefits (FEMA, 2020a).

[1] A precalculated benefit is a standardized unit cost per physical unit of measure. For example, FEMA has established a precalculated benefit of $323,000 for the acquisition of a repetitive loss or severe repetitive loss of property as defined by the National Flood Insurance Program.

Changes are also being driven by updated policy and guidance from the executive branch. Two 2021 executive orders (EOs) recognized the past inequities of federal investment and provide guidance to all federal agencies to remedy such actions going forward. In EO 14008, signed in January 2021, "Tackling the Climate Crisis at Home and Abroad," President Joseph R. Biden, Jr., established the Justice40 Initiative, directing federal agencies to achieve greater equity and fairness in allocating federal resources, indicating specifically that "40 percent of the overall benefits" of certain federal investments must "flow to disadvantaged communities." Interim implementation guidance for the Justice40 Initiative selected two HMA programs—Building Resilient Infrastructure and Communities (BRIC) and Flood Mitigation Assistance (FMA)—as pilot programs (Young, Mallory, and McCarthy, 2021).

Additional guidance related to equity considerations comes from EO 13985, also signed in January 2021, "Advancing Racial Equity and Support for Underserved Communities Through the Federal Government," which provides a blueprint for a whole-of-government approach to identifying barriers that underserved communities face in accessing federal programs.[2]

As FEMA charts a course forward, it can consider guidance from these EOs and from its own National Advisory Council (NAC). The NAC's 2020 report to the FEMA administrator (NAC, 2020) includes multiple recommendations about building national capacity for equitable solutions in the field of emergency management. The NAC also recognizes the BCA's role in perpetuating inequity in access to grant funding. In its 2021 report to the FEMA administrator, the NAC recommended that FEMA consider using a reduced BCA discount rate, arguing that the higher discount rate acts as a barrier that restricts some communities' ability to access FEMA funding.[3] FEMA responded that "FEMA recognizes that the 7% discount rate makes achieving a positive BCA challenging for some communities and projects, is actively exploring efficiencies for the BCA requirement, and is committed to easing the burden for communities" (Criswell, 2022, p. 16). Specifically, FEMA is concerned that a 7-percent discount rate exceeds the true future discount rate for many communities and thereby underestimates long-run benefits relative to up-front costs, resulting in an erroneously low BCR. However, FEMA reports that it has historically deferred to OMB officials in maintaining a 7-percent discount rate to projects, as advised by OMB Circular A-94.[4] The extent to which the choice of interest rates disproportionately prevents lower-resourced or less urban communities from accessing HMA funds is not clear. Regardless, the ideal discount rate would accurately reflect the present value of future costs and benefits to that community.

FEMA's goal is to increase equity of access and delivery of mitigation grant programs by reducing complexity while also considering potential benefits more broadly. To support this goal, FEMA seeks to explore changes that might expand lower-resourced communities' access to these resilience dollars while still meeting the cost-effectiveness requirements of the Stafford Act, its corresponding regulations, and executive branch policies. Reducing the administrative costs associated with submitting subapplications might increase participation by communities that might otherwise find the application process cost-prohibitive. Furthermore,

---

[2] *Underserved community* refers to a community that faces barriers in accessing and using services provided by physical or social systems and includes populations underserved for diverse reasons (e.g., geographic isolation, race or ethnicity, age, gender, language barriers, or low income or wealth level).

[3] Specifically, the NAC stated,

> Continued use of the high 7% discount rate favors jurisdictions with: a) the resources to maximize the arduous BCA methodology and b) jurisdictions with dense and expensive built environments. The fixed 7% discount rate has set an effective barrier to the participation of smaller jurisdictions. Those applicants without a dense and expensive built environment are mathematically unable to accumulate sufficient large benefits (damages averted in the BCA methodology) to withstand 30–50 years of discounting to the present value at a 7% rate. This barrier runs contrary to the administration's equity policies and the intent of mitigation programs. (NAC, 2021, pp. 25–26)

[4] FEMA staff, conversations with HSOAC researchers, June 2022. As discussed in Chapter 4, officials from different federal entities had different views on the extent to which alternative discount rates could be employed.

changes that incorporate broader categories of benefits that are not currently included in BCA methodology might help identify and support subapplicants that are inequitably served by the current methodology.

FEMA is also facing simultaneous and potentially conflicting pressures to make the BCA process more data-rich and robust. FEMA staff report that OMB officials have requested increasingly detailed sensitivity analyses of the assumptions and other inputs used in the BCA process and that FEMA should apply a 7-percent discount rate to projects, which reduces the monetized value of benefits that accrue further into the future or over many years and could cause some projects to fall short of a BCR of 1 or greater.[5]

Although FEMA has successfully implemented some adjustments to the BCA process, these generally represent marginal changes to the existing BCA approaches rather than a fundamentally different approach to how the requirements of the Stafford Act are met. In this study, we explored whether alternative interpretations or methodologies might improve FEMA's ability to effectively and efficiently implement mitigation programs while considering issues of equity and simultaneously comply with the Stafford Act, its corresponding regulations, and executive branch policies.

Approach and Outline of This Report

To undertake this study, the HSOAC team engaged in multiple research tasks, which we describe in the relevant chapters, as follows:

- We began by reviewing FEMA's current BCA methodology (Chapter 2).
- We then examined the literature documenting challenges the current approach presents to subapplicants and the literature related to potential alternatives or changes to the BCA process, in all cases with a focus on disadvantaged communities (Chapter 3).
- We then reviewed the authorities that dictate how the BCA process must function as represented by the legal, regulatory, and policy frameworks under which the grant programs are administered (Chapter 4).
- Finally, we spoke with representatives of other federal agencies that use BCA processes in administering nonregulatory grant programs and benchmarked the requirements and methodologies of those grant programs relative to FEMA's grant programs (Chapter 5).

We conclude the report by using the findings from these analyses to identify potential alternative approaches that could be relevant for FEMA to improve equity of access to HMA grants while still meeting legal and regulatory requirements (see Chapter 6). In the appendix, we also reproduce the protocol we used during our interviews.

---

[5] FEMA staff, conversations with HSOAC researchers, November 2021.

CHAPTER 2

FEMA Hazard Mitigation Assistance Grant Programs

In this chapter, we provide an overview of FEMA's current HMA grant programs and review FEMA's current BCA methodology. We also describe how BCA does and does not mechanically enter into decisions about how to allocate funding and how incentives, in turn, influence the BCAs submitted by subapplicants. These discussions are based on our review of documentation and literature associated with each of the HMA grant programs, analysis of HMA grant program data, and discussions with relevant FEMA staff.

Current FEMA Hazard Mitigation Assistance Grant Programs

FEMA administers multiple grant programs that fall into the category of HMA or HMA programs. These are the Hazard Mitigation Grant Program (HMGP), the FMA program, and BRIC. The communities that develop and intend to carry out mitigation projects are often referred to as *subapplicants* because these communities must apply through designated applicants, which are typically states, territories, or federally recognized tribes (FEMA, 2015). An applicant submits one application to FEMA that might consist of multiple subapplications. A subapplicant might need to go through a screening process established by an applicant before the applicant will forward the subapplication to FEMA for consideration.[1]

HMGP is the oldest of the three HMA programs. State, local, territorial, and tribal governments may apply for HMGP funding following a presidentially declared disaster (or, for Post Fire funding, following award of a Fire Management Assistance Grant) to enable communities to rebuild to be less vulnerable to hazards in the future (FEMA, 2021a). Funding offered to these communities through HMGP comes from the DRF. The maximum amount of HMGP funding available to a community in response to a given disaster declaration is based on a percentage of the total federal assistance made through other FEMA programs.[2] HMGP is not a competitive program, although applicants must still meet a variety of eligibility criteria, which include cost-effectiveness (FEMA, 2021a). A notable caveat is the 5 Percent Initiative, an HMGP set-aside that allocates as much as 5 percent of HMGP funds for mitigation projects that are "difficult to evaluate using FEMA-approved cost effectiveness methodologies" (FEMA, 2015, p. 111). An applicant under the 5 Percent Initiative must provide a narrative justification of cost-effectiveness but does not need to submit a BCA.

FMA is a competitive grant program designed to reduce or eliminate flood damage risks, specifically by providing funds to applicants for projects that mitigate flood damage to buildings insured under the National

---

[1] Structural differences in applicants' processes can influence advancement of project subapplications from the applicant to FEMA. However, FEMA has little insight into the applicant process (FEMA staff, conversations with HSOAC researchers, June 2022).

[2] At present, the HMGP cap is based on 15 percent of the total expenditures by certain Public Assistance and Individual Assistance programs. For exceptionally large disasters, such as Hurricane Maria, which hit Puerto Rico and the U.S. Virgin Islands in 2017, the funding amount is capped at an amount known as the *lock-in ceiling* (Code of Federal Regulations [C.F.R.], Title 44, Section 207.2). HMGP also covers management costs that do not count against these caps (FEMA staff, communications with the authors, August 29, 2022).

Flood Insurance Program (NFIP) (FEMA, 2022g). Unlike HMGP, the FMA program focuses only on flood hazard mitigation. In fiscal year (FY) 2020, $160 million was available for FMA grants, and, in FY 2021, $200 million was available (Horn, 2022). In FY 2022, FMA funding jumped to $800 million (FEMA, 2022a).

BRIC is the newest HMA program and provides funds to states, local communities, tribes, and territories to reduce or eliminate disaster and natural hazard risks. As shown in Figure 2.1, the BRIC program represents a notable increase in FEMA predisaster HMA funding, and the numbers of subapplications for competitive BRIC and FMA funding exceeded available funds by factors of four and three, respectively, in FY 2021. The BRIC program was first authorized by the Disaster Recovery Reform Act of 2018 (Pub. L. 115-254, Division D).

In FY 2020 and FY 2021, the first two years of program implementation, $500 million and $1 billion, respectively, of BRIC funds were made available. Of these totals, $446.4 million and $919 million were accessible through the national competition, a process in which subapplications from U.S. states, territories, and federally recognized tribes are submitted for project funding. A competitive evaluation process determines which projects are selected for funding (FEMA, 2021c; HMA Division, 2020). The BRIC funds awarded outside of the national competition are composed of allocations to states, territories, and federally recognized tribes. BRIC has the potential to grow much larger because the authorizing legislation allows the president to set aside up to 6 percent of the DRF.[3] BRIC funding for FY 2022 was $2.3 billion (White House, 2022).

FIGURE 2.1

Funding for Predisaster Hazard Mitigation, Fiscal Years 1997 Through 2022

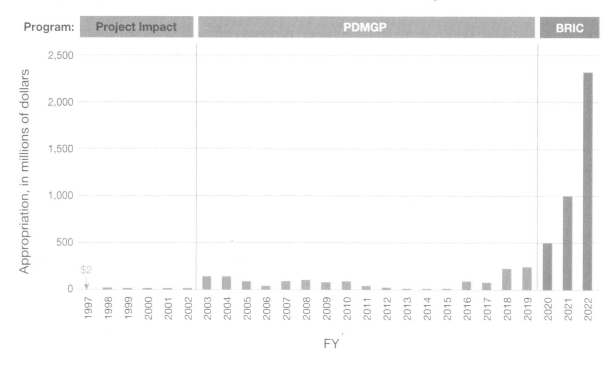

SOURCES: Horn, 2022; White House, 2022.

---

[3] Section 1234 of the Disaster Recovery Reform Act of 2018 (Pub. L. 115-254, Div. D) authorized national public infrastructure PDM assistance, which, at the president's discretion, can be funded with up to a 6-percent set-aside from disaster expenditures made through U.S. Code, Title 42, Sections 5170b, 5172, 5173, 5174, 5177, 5183, and 5189g.

According to the U.S. Government Accountability Office (GAO), from FY 2010–FY 2018 approximately 88 percent of FEMA hazard mitigation funding was awarded after the disaster (GAO, 2021).[4] The BRIC program represents a notable shift toward more proactive, rather than reactive, hazard mitigation investment by FEMA. In FY 2021, a single BRIC subapplication could request up to $50 million in federal cost share. BRIC replaces the Pre-Disaster Mitigation Grant Program (PDMGP), which no longer awards funds to new projects and was FEMA's primary program for awarding predisaster hazard mitigation funding from FY 2003–FY 2019. In FY 2019, PDMGP awarded $250 million in funding for predisaster hazard mitigation projects, half of the FY 2020 appropriation for BRIC and one-quarter of BRIC's FY 2021 appropriation (FEMA, 2023).

Table 2.1 lists the names of the HMA programs, the years in which they were established, their activating mechanisms, and their FY 2021 funding amounts. Tables 2.2 through 2.4 describe eligibility criteria for HMA program applicants, subapplicants, and projects, as well as typical project types.

Cost-Effectiveness Assessment in Hazard Mitigation Assistance Programs

In order to meet HMA programs' cost-effectiveness eligibility requirement, a subapplicant must submit a BCA or alternative documentation demonstrating cost-effectiveness.[5] For a project to be considered cost-effective, it must have a BCR that is greater than or equal to 1. FEMA provides software to help applicants

TABLE 2.1

Hazard Mitigation Assistance Programs

Program	Year Established	Activating Mechanism	FY 2021 Funding, in Millions of Dollars
HMGP	1988 (Pub L. 93-288)	PD	1,157[a]
FMA	1994 (FEMA, 2007)	Available without declaration, but eligible applicants and subapplicants must participate in the NFIP (FEMA, 2021e)	160
BRIC[b]	2020 (FEMA, 2020b)	PD in the seven years prior to the annual grant application period start date[c]	1,000
HMGP Post Fire	2018 (FEMA, 2022i)	PD or any area affected by a fire for which assistance was provided under Section 420 of the Stafford Act.	33.4[a]

NOTE: PD = presidential declaration. FY 2021 funding amounts confirmed through communications with FEMA on August 29, 2022.

[a] Because of the nature of the HMGP, the amount of funds obligated to various disasters in a given FY is not the same as the amount of HMGP funding for which a community becomes eligible because of disasters that occur in that FY. This table reflects that, in total, $1.157 billion in HMGP funding and $33.4 million in HMGP Post Fire funding was obligated in FY 2021 across qualifying disasters that occurred across multiple years. For comparison, communities became eligible for approximately $980 million in HMGP funds and approximately $28.6 million in HMGP Post Fire funds in FY 2021. This was down from FY 2020 levels, in which communities became eligible for approximately $3.8 billion in HMGP funds and $50.1 million in HMGP Post Fire funds. These values can sometimes adjust slightly as funding from other programs is finalized (FEMA staff, communications with the authors, August 29, 2022).

[b] BRIC was first implemented in FY 2020, and it is the successor to FEMA's PDMGP, which was in place from FY 2003 to FY 2019. The priorities of the BRIC program are not identical to those of PDMGP. PDMGP was preceded by Project Impact, which ran from FY 1997–FY 2002. See McCarthy and Keegan (2009).

[c] According to FEMA, all states, territories, tribes, and the District of Columbia met this requirement as of June 2022 because of the coronavirus disease 2019 (COVID-19) pandemic that triggered a nationwide presidential disaster declaration (FEMA, 2021e).

---

[4] This calculation includes other FEMA programs that provide both disaster assistance and hazard mitigation funding, such as the Public Assistance Program.

[5] FEMA's BCA team reports that virtually all subapplicants use the BCA rather than an alternative approach.

TABLE 2.2
Flood Mitigation Assistance Program Eligibility and Projects

Category	Criterion
Applicant	An applicant can be a state, the District of Columbia, U.S. territory, or federally recognized tribal government.
	Each state, the District of Columbia, territory, and federally recognized tribal government shall designate one agency to serve as the applicant for funding. Each applicant's designated agency may submit only one FMA grant application to FEMA. An application can be made up of an unlimited number of subapplications.
	Each applicant must have a FEMA-approved state or tribal hazard mitigation plan by the application deadline and at the time of obligation of grant funds.
Subapplicant	A subapplicant is a local government (i.e., city, township, county, special district government) or a state agency or federally recognized tribal government that chooses to apply as a subapplicant. Each must submit its subapplication to its state, territory, or tribal applicant agency.
	Every subapplicant for FMA must be participating in the NFIP and not be withdrawn or suspended.
	Every subapplicant must have a FEMA-approved local or tribal hazard mitigation plan by the application deadline and at the time of obligation of grant funds for mitigation projects (with the exception of mitigation planning).
	A federally recognized tribal government or non–federally recognized tribes can choose to apply as a subapplicant with an eligible state or territory as the applicant.
Project	A project must • be cost-effective • be in good standing in a participating NFIP community • align with the applicable hazard mitigation plan • meet all EHP requirements. Example projects are • Project scoping • Technical assistance • Community flood mitigation project • Individual structure or property-level flood mitigation project • Management cost

SOURCE: Descriptions confirmed through FEMA staff, communications with the authors, July 2022.
NOTE: EHP = environmental and historic preservation.

calculate their BCRs.[6] The applicant quantifies the benefits of the project, such as the amount of damage avoided during events with particular return frequencies (i.e., the expected monetary damage averted in an event that happens every five years or every 20 years), and the project useful life (PUL), which is the duration of time over which those benefits are assumed to occur. Based on this information, the tool automatically calculates the expected annual benefits in each year of the PUL, then calculates the present value of those benefits by applying a future discount rate (this rate has traditionally been the 7-percent rate prescribed in OMB Circular A-94). On the cost side, the applicant provides (1) a single, lump-sum value for project costs and (2) the annualized cost of any ongoing maintenance requirements. The lump-sum project cost is not limited to construction costs; it includes broader considerations, such as land acquisition and management costs. The present value of costs is then calculated as the lump-sum project cost (which is not subject to future discounting[7]) plus the present value of annual maintenance costs (which are subject to the same discount rate as benefits are). The BCR is then calculated as the ratio of the present value of benefits to the present value of costs.

---

[6] The following discussion of how BCRs are calculated is based on author discussions with FEMA staff on September 29, 2022.

[7] Because these costs are not discounted, the present value of costs could be overestimated when these costs are spread across multiple years. The treatment of costs mirrors how FEMA allocates awarded HMA funds, which are provided as a single lump

TABLE 2.3

Building Resilient Infrastructure and Communities Eligibility and Projects

Category	Criterion
Applicant	It must meet the same criteria as for the FMA program and • if it is a state or territory, it must have received a major disaster declaration under the Stafford Act in the seven years prior to the annual grant application period start date. • if it is a federally recognized tribal government, it must have received a major disaster declaration under the Stafford Act in the seven years prior to the annual grant application period start date or be entirely or partially located in a state that received a major disaster declaration during this period.
Subapplicant	It must meet the same criteria as for the FMA program and • if it is a tribal government requesting to apply through the state, the state must have received a major disaster declaration under the Stafford Act in the seven years prior to the annual grant application period start date.
Project	A project must • be cost-effective • reduce or eliminate risk and damage from future natural hazards • meet either of the two latest published editions of relevant consensus-based building codes, specifications, and standards • align with applicable hazard mitigation plans • meet all EHP requirements. Example projects are • Capability- and capacity-building activity • Mitigation project • Management cost

SOURCE: Descriptions confirmed through FEMA staff, communications with the authors, July 2022.

The BCR does not directly influence project prioritization once the project has met the cost-effectiveness requirement. Subapplications are evaluated and prioritized across a variety of criteria, but the BCR directly factors only into whether a subapplication is deemed eligible. As discussed in Chapter 5, FEMA HMA programs' cost-effectiveness criterion contrasts with other agencies' approaches, such as the U.S. Army Corps of Engineers (USACE) civil works mission of developing and selecting projects with the objective of maximizing national net benefits (Durden and Fredericks, 2009).

The HMA cost-effectiveness criterion is not designed to direct funds to projects that reduce the greatest hazard risk. Subapplications with higher BCRs do not explicitly receive higher priority for funding once eligibility has been determined. Subapplications are evaluated for eligibility and completeness, and cost-effectiveness is one eligibility criterion. Because the total amount of funding requests received by HMA programs typically exceeds program budgets, there are cases in which eligible subapplications (e.g., those with BCRs greater than 1 and meeting other eligibility criteria) are not selected for awards.[8] Following determination of eligibility and completeness, competitive FMA and BRIC subapplications are scored according to technical and qualitative criteria developed by FEMA,[9] which directly influence project prioritization and ranking. A subapplication will receive one of three responses from FEMA: (1) did not meet HMA requirements, (2) was not selected, or (3) was selected for further review, which generally means that the project has been selected for funding (FEMA, 2015). Figure 2.2 illustrates the flow of competitive subapplications through the FY 2020 BRIC program application cycle.

---

sum rather than spread out over time.

[8] For example, in FY 2020, the BRIC program received 568 competitive subapplications submitted in connection with the national competition, and only 22 were selected for further review.

[9] The criteria are identified each year in the notice of funding opportunity. The criteria can vary from year to year to reflect specific priorities.

TABLE 2.4

Hazard Mitigation Grant Program Eligibility and Projects

Category	Criterion
Applicant (same as for FMA)	An applicant can be a state, the District of Columbia, U.S. territory, or federally recognized tribal government.
	Each state, the District of Columbia, territory, and federally recognized tribal government shall designate one agency to serve as the applicant for funding. Each applicant's designated agency may submit only one HMGP grant application to FEMA. An application can be made up of an unlimited number of subapplications.
	Each applicant must have a FEMA-approved state or tribal hazard mitigation plan by the application deadline and at the time of obligation of grant funds.
Subapplicant (same as for FMA)	A subapplicant is a local government (i.e., city, township, county, special district government) or a state agency or federally recognized tribal government that chooses to apply as a subapplicant. Each must submit its subapplication to its state, territory, or tribal applicant agency.
	Every subapplicant for HMGP must be participating in the NFIP and not be withdrawn or suspended.
	Every subapplicant must have a FEMA-approved local or tribal hazard mitigation plan by the application deadline and at the time of obligation of grant funds for mitigation projects (with the exception of mitigation planning).
	A federally recognized tribal government or non–federally recognized tribe can choose to apply as a subapplicant with an eligible state or territory as the applicant.
Project	A project must • be cost-effective • align with the applicable hazard mitigation plan • meet all EHP requirements. Example projects are • Retrofitting an existing building to reduce vulnerability to natural hazards • Purchasing hazard-prone property to remove people and structures from harm's way • Utility or infrastructure retrofit to reduce risk of failure • Drainage improvement project to reduce potential for flood damage • Slope stabilization project to reduce risk to people and structures • Developing and adopting a hazard mitigation plan, which is required for state, local, territorial, and tribal governments to receive funding for their hazard mitigation projects • Using aquifer storage and recovery, floodplain and stream restoration, flood diversion and storage, or green infrastructure methods to reduce the impacts of flood and drought

SOURCE: Descriptions confirmed through FEMA staff, communications with the authors, July 2022.

Each project carries a variety of potential benefits, with constraints placed on what can be counted as project benefits. The first stipulation is that all benefits must be quantifiable; benefits that cannot be monetized can be described but do not count toward the BCR (FEMA, 2019a). Moreover, some project impacts, such as economic growth realized thanks to avoided damage, reduced emissions, and energy cost savings, do not count as project benefits (FEMA, 2019a). Avoided losses that may be included as benefits include avoided physical damage, loss of service or function, injuries and deaths, displacement costs, emergency management costs, and NFIP administration costs. A project might also incorporate ecosystem service benefits (HMA Division, 2021b) and social benefits to increase its BCR, although the latter may be included only if the BCR is already 0.75 or greater (FEMA, 2019b). In this context, FEMA defines *social benefits* as "avoided costs associated with mental stress and anxiety and lost wages that disaster survivors would otherwise experience" (FEMA, 2019b, p. 21). Some benefits are counted only for certain project types—such as avoided mortality, which can be incorporated in benefit calculations for tornado safe rooms, hurricane safe rooms, and seismic retrofit projects (FEMA, 2019b). According to FEMA staff, some benefits, such as avoided mortality, are considered across hazard and project types; however, benefits from these components are not included for all hazards in the BCA Toolkit, a decision made by FEMA.

FIGURE 2.2

Idealized Flow of Subapplications Within the Fiscal Year 2020 Building Resilient Infrastructure and Communities Competition

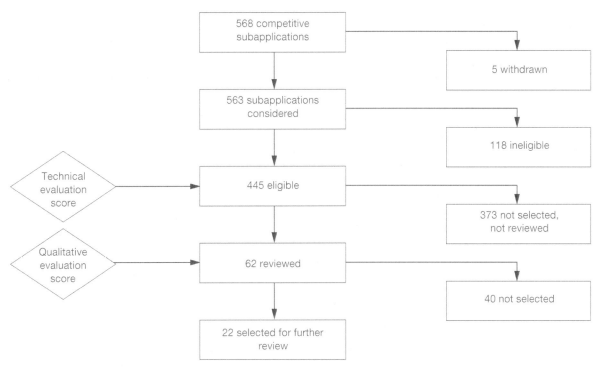

SOURCE: Finucane et al., forthcoming.

Other inputs to the BCA calculator will affect the value of a project's net benefits. The PUL is the number of years over which benefits are calculated. Sometimes this is automatically provided by certain mitigation activities, but in cases in which the proposed PUL exceeds the "acceptable limit" specified by the BCA Toolkit, subapplicants and applicants might need to justify the PUL by providing "documented assurances" that the project will be maintained for the proposed amount of time (FEMA, 2022c). For example, floodplain and stream restoration projects have a maximum PUL of 30 years, suggesting that benefits beyond this 30-year time horizon are discounted so heavily they have been eliminated from consideration altogether. Some scholars and policy experts have commented that fully valuing the long-term benefits of resilience projects might address intergenerational equity (Parker and Ritter, 2021; President's State, Local, and Tribal Leaders Task Force on Climate Preparedness and Resilience, 2014; Weitzman, 1998), and expanding the scope of certain HMA projects' PUL is one potential pathway by which FEMA might address these intergenerational equity concerns. Additionally, calculation of the present value of a project's future benefits relies not only on PUL but on the discount rate as well. Lowering (increasing) the discount rate or expanding (reducing) the PUL can increase (decrease) the present value of future project benefits. This issue is discussed in more detail in Chapters 5 and 6.

Confirmation from Fiscal Year 2020 Building Resilient Infrastructure and Communities Data

The use of BCR as an eligibility criterion rather than a factor that influences funding allocations means that the BCA is, in practice, better described as a threshold analysis. Indeed, some nonprofit organizations and companies (e.g., Environmental Defense Fund and AECOM) explicitly advise applicants and subapplicants that the BCA is a "threshold criterion" (Environmental Defense Fund, 2022).

Subapplicants appear to be largely aware of this incentive structure and adjust their behavior accordingly. In this section, we describe analysis conducted on data from FY 2020 BRIC applications, which confirms the statements made earlier in this chapter. Data on the BCR of selected HMA projects in Figure 2.3 and the BCR of all FY 2020 BRIC applications in Figure 2.4 suggest that most applicants do not calculate a BCR significantly higher than 1, even though independent estimates of the average savings due to such federal PDM programs range from $4 to $6 of averted losses per $1 spent (Godschalk et al., 2009; Multi-Hazard Mitigation Council, 2019).

If a subapplication does not exhaustively enumerate associated project benefits once the cost-effectiveness criterion has been met, some benefits might be left uncalculated. This creates multiple challenges. First, if benefits are not being fully captured, it will not be possible to determine whether Justice40's objective of 40 percent of benefits going to disadvantaged communities is being met. Second, it will not be possible to ensure that program funding goes to the projects with the highest net benefit. However, as discussed in both this chapter and Chapter 3, the current award process is not necessarily designed to direct funding to projects with the greatest net benefit. Figure 2.5 presents FY 2020 BRIC subapplication submission BCRs and confirms that, among projects that have met the cost-effectiveness criterion, projects with higher BCR scores are not necessarily prioritized for subapplication selection. Figure 2.6 presents the BCRs of FY 2020 BRIC subapplications selected for further review (winning subapplications), although, as described above, the reported BCR might not reflect the project's true net benefits.

Summary of Findings

In this chapter, we have provided an overview of FEMA's current HMA grant programs, FEMA's current BCA methodology, how BCA does and does not mechanically enter into decisions about how to allocate

FIGURE 2.3

Distribution of Fiscal Year 2020 Hazard Mitigation Assistance Subapplication BCRs

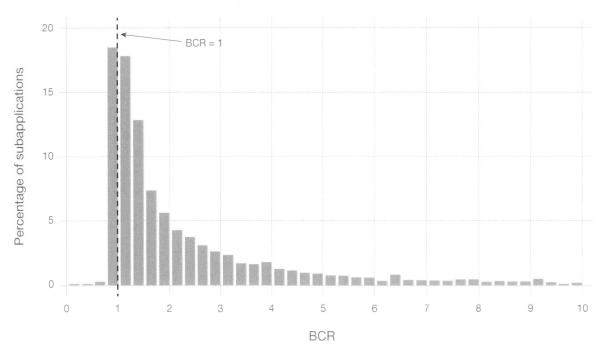

FIGURE 2.4

Fiscal Year 2020 Building Resilient Infrastructure and Communities Subapplication BCRs

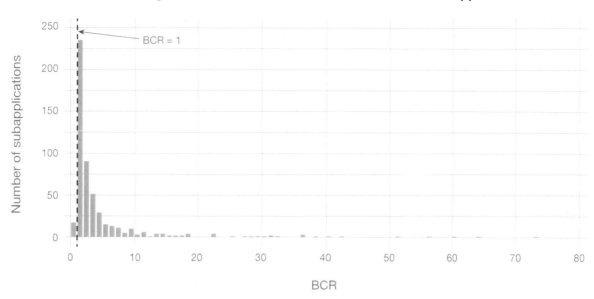

NOTE: In FY 2020, BRIC received a total of 991 subapplications, 568 of which were in the competitive funding category. Of the 568 competitive subapplications, 525 had BCRs less than 0.75, which are shown in the figure (applications with BCRs above 0.75 are excluded from this figure for legibility purposes). The red dashed vertical line represents a BCR of 1.0.

funding, and how those factors, in turn, influence the BCAs submitted by subapplicants. The key findings are as follows:

- FEMA administers three grant programs in the HMA category: HMGP, the FMA program, and BRIC.
- Communities that develop and intend to carry out mitigation projects are referred to as *subapplicants*, and these communities must apply through designated applicants, which are typically states, territories, or federally recognized tribes. An applicant submits one application to FEMA that may consist of multiple subapplications.
- HMGP is the oldest of the three HMA programs and offers project funding to state, local, territorial, and tribal governments after a presidentially declared disaster to enable communities to rebuild to be less vulnerable to hazards in the future.
- The FMA program is designed to reduce or eliminate flood damage risks, specifically by providing funds to applicants for projects that mitigate flood damage to buildings insured under the NFIP.
- BRIC is the newest HMA program and provides funds to states, local communities, tribes, and territories to reduce or eliminate disaster and natural hazard risks. The BRIC program represents a notable increase in FEMA predisaster hazard mitigation assistance funding: For FY 2020 and FY 2021, the first two years of program implementation, $500 million and $1 billion, respectively, of BRIC funds were made available. For FY 2022, BRIC funding was increased to $2.3 billion.
- Subapplications for competitive BRIC and FMA funding exceeded available funds by factors of four and three, respectively, in FY 2021, suggesting robust demand for competitive HMA program funds.
- To meet HMA programs' cost-effectiveness eligibility requirement, a subapplication must submit a BCA or alternative documentation demonstrating cost-effectiveness. For a project to be considered cost-effective, it must have a BCR that is greater than or equal to 1, indicating that the present value of project benefits exceed costs.

FIGURE 2.5

Fiscal Year 2020 Building Resilient Infrastructure and Communities Subapplication BCRs, by Selection Status

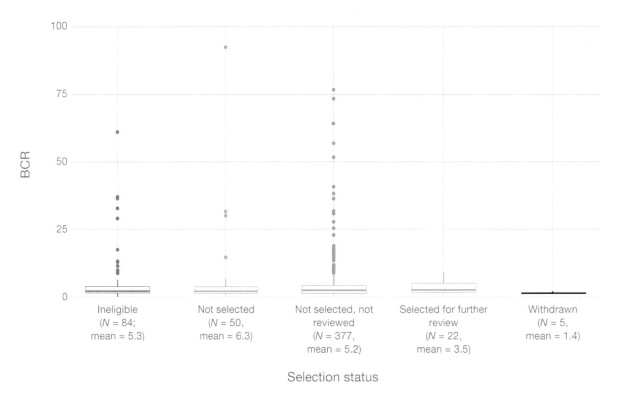

NOTE: In FY 2020, BRIC received a total of 991 subapplications, 568 of which were in the competitive funding category. Of the 568 competitive subapplications, 34 were missing BCR data. This plot shows subapplications with BCRs below 100.

- Constraints are placed on what can be counted as project benefits, and all benefits must be quantifiable. Besides economic benefits, a project may incorporate ecosystem service benefits and social benefits to increase its BCR, although the latter may be included only if the BCR is already 0.75 or greater.
- Although cost-effectiveness is an eligibility criterion for projects funded by HMA programs, subapplications are not prioritized for funding according to level of cost-effectiveness. This fact explains why both interviews with FEMA staff and analysis of FY 2020 BRIC subapplication data suggest that many BRIC subapplicants tend to submit BCAs with BCRs slightly above 1.

FIGURE 2.6

Fiscal Year 2020 BCRs of Building Resilient Infrastructure and Communities Subapplications Selected for Further Review

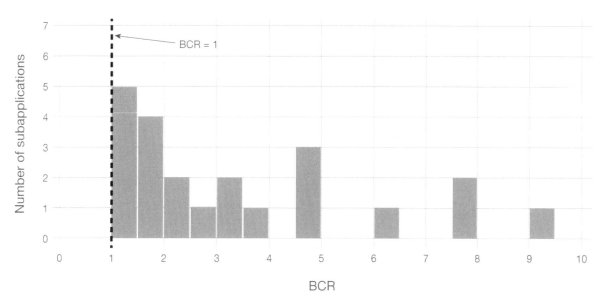

NOTE: In FY 2020, BRIC received a total of 991 subapplications, 568 of which were in the competitive funding category. Of the 568 competitive subapplications, 22 were selected for further review, the final stage of the selection process.

CHAPTER 3

Equity in Hazard Mitigation Grant Programs

Chapter 2 provided a broad overview of FEMA's HMA programs and described how BCA does and does not mechanically enter into decisions about how to allocate funding. This chapter discusses concerns about inequities in the allocations of HMA funding, the ways in which equity is currently incorporated into HMA programs, and considerations for further incorporating equity into HMA programs' cost-effectiveness assessments.

Equity in Hazard Mitigation Assistance Programs

Equity Concerns

Many recent reports—both from academia and from the media—have presented evidence of inequities in the ultimate distribution of FEMA response and grant funding, including HMA funding. In some cases, the BCA process is blamed for propagating such inequities, both in the context of FEMA programs and more generally.[1] Yet, as discussed in Chapter 2, the BCA process does not consider "distributional factors,"[2] such as how benefits are distributed by income, geographical region, or demographic group, and BCA is not directly considered in funding determinations beyond its role in determining eligibility. Although BCA does not explicitly consider how HMA benefits are distributed in determining cost-effectiveness, such factors are explicitly considered as part of FEMA's procedures for selecting which competitive HMA subapplications will be funded.

These observations can make simultaneous discussion of BCAs and equity confusing to follow. The relevant links between the two issues are ultimately captured by two concerns, both of which are important but neither of which has, to our knowledge, been clearly and systematically confirmed or disproven by objective empirical evidence.

The first link between BCA and equity is a concern that some communities might have greater difficulty than others in meeting the BCR eligibility threshold. There is concern that the types of benefits most relevant to disadvantaged communities might be more difficult to quantify or might not be eligible benefits. The second link between BCA and equity is a concern that the complexity and difficulty of conducting a BCA discourage lower-resourced communities from applying at all, regardless of whether there are differences in

---

[1] For examples, see Goodwin (2020) and Headwaters Economics (2021b).

[2] OMB Circular A-94 does not define *distributional effects*; however, it includes guidance on how to evaluate them:

> Distributional effects may be analyzed by grouping individuals or households according to income class (e.g., income quintiles), geographical region, or demographic group (e.g., age). Other classifications, such as by industry or occupation, may be appropriate in some circumstances.

> Analysis should aim at identifying the relevant gainers and losers from policy decisions. Effects on the preexisting assignment of property rights by the program under analysis should be reported. Where a policy is intended to benefit a specified subgroup of the population, such as the poor, the analysis should consider how effective the policy is in reaching its targeted group. (p. 12)

difficulty across communities. Indeed, applicants and subapplicants to the HMA grant programs have provided extensive feedback that the BCA process is cumbersome and that finding the right data to include in the calculations of costs and benefits is difficult. If certain groups or communities are more or less likely to apply for funding, because of either BCA-related challenges or other differences in ability to access or pursue subapplications, the ultimate distribution of funding might reflect inequities that are already present in the pool of subapplications.

FEMA's Current Procedures

As discussed in Chapter 1, FEMA is concerned that administrative burden and the costs of application processes could discourage subapplicants with fewer resources from applying or place them at a disadvantage in developing quality applications. As of FY 2022, FEMA had sought to address this concern by providing assistance in completing BCAs to BRIC and FMA subapplicants with Social Vulnerability Index (SVI) scores of 0.8 or greater (HMA Division, 2022). And EO 14008 and EO 13985 have directed federal agencies to achieve greater equity and fairness in allocating federal resources. Two of the HMA grant programs, BRIC and FMA, have been selected as pilot programs for the corresponding federalwide initiative known as Justice40 (Young, Mallory, and McCarthy, 2021). This chapter explores the important challenges, nuances, and context that should be considered in efforts to address inequities in FEMA's distribution of HMA grants.

FEMA's current procedures for selecting which competitive HMA subapplications will be funded give substantial consideration to distributional priorities, although not within the BCA process. For example, when considering FMA subapplications, FEMA has now begun awarding points based on census tract–level Centers for Disease Control and Prevention (CDC) SVI scores of subapplications across project types (HMA Division, 2021a).[3] In the BRIC program's national competition, distributional factors are weighted in components of both technical and qualitative criteria (FEMA, 2022k; FEMA, 2022l). Specifically, technical criterion 8, designation as an economically disadvantaged rural community (EDRC), can yield up to 15 points (out of 115 possible points for technical criteria) to subapplicants qualifying as EDRCs under U.S. Code, Title 42, Section 5133(a), although this EDRC definition is distinct from other definitions of *disadvantaged community* relevant to HMA programs, as discussed later in this chapter and in Chapter 4 (FEMA, 2021f). BRIC qualitative criterion 1, risk reduction and resilience effectiveness, which accounts for 35 out of 100 possible points for qualitative criteria, may award points to subapplications if they demonstrate ancillary benefits that "address inequities and provide the greatest support to those with greatest need" (FEMA, 2021b). Additionally, qualitative criterion 4, population impacted, which accounts for 15 out of the 100 possible points for qualitative criteria, awards points if the subapplication directly benefits a "disadvantaged community" as referenced in EO 14008 (FEMA, 2021b). Thus, distributional factors do have significant weight in evaluation of competitive HMA subapplications. The consideration of these distributional factors, like all factors used to select which eligible projects receive funding, is separate and subsequent to the use of BCA to determine eligibility based on cost-effectiveness.

For all HMA programs, communities do not apply directly to FEMA but rather to applicants (e.g., states, territories, federally recognized tribes). Applicants are charged with both administering the program and prioritizing which subapplications from within their jurisdictions are forwarded to FEMA for review and approval (FEMA, 2016). Because states, territories, and federally recognized tribes control which subapplica-

---

[3] For capability- and capacity-building activities, which support the development or updating of multihazard mitigation plans, up to ten of the 22 total points are based on the average SVI of all census tracts included in the benefiting area. For localized flood risk reduction projects, up to 200 of 1,040 points are awarded based on the average SVI of all census tracts included in a benefiting area.

tions are submitted to FEMA, they have substantial influence over which subapplications ultimately receive HMA funding.

Challenges Associated with Conducting BCAs

All HMA subapplications must demonstrate cost-effectiveness to be eligible for HMA program funding. FEMA's BCA reference guide advises applicants and subapplicants to accomplish this by developing and integrating BCA or other documentation demonstrating cost-effectiveness into the subapplication (FEMA, 2009). In practice, this means that smaller, lower-resourced subapplicants often shoulder the burden of collecting and producing the technical information needed to satisfy these application requirements. Some of the information required to compile a complete and competitive subapplication, such as the engineering feasibility or the cost-effectiveness requirement, demands a substantial amount of technical expertise, staff time, and data that could be prohibitive for applicants and subapplicants with limited resources and capacity (GAO, 2021). These issues can be exacerbated by poor data quality—especially in estimating historical hazard recurrence intervals—further necessitating oversight from engineers or other experts (FEMA, 2011). In the case of BRIC, the distribution of awarded funds so far has varied substantially across states, territories, and tribes, with a handful of states on the east and west coasts slated to receive 90 percent of all FY 2020 BRIC funds.[4] Some of these disparities could be driven by varying levels of support and technical capacity across applicants and subapplicants in that certain applicants (e.g., the District of Columbia) and subapplicants provide targeted financial support to increase the competitiveness of HMA subapplications under their management (Government of the District of Columbia, 2021). Differences in communities' levels of exposure to natural hazards could also influence the ease with which they can meet BCR requirements and hence the distribution of HMA grants. These factors, and others, could contribute to uneven allocation of competitive HMA program funds. Further study of the roles these factors play could help FEMA's HMA programs not only to reduce the country's overall risk portfolio but also to do so in an equitable manner.

FEMA is aware of the difficulty of conducting a full BCA and has made efforts to ease the burden on applicants and subapplicants. Most prominent is FEMA's creation of the publicly available BCA Toolkit, a Microsoft Excel add-in that allows users to more easily calculate project costs and benefits using FEMA-approved methodologies and precalculated benefits (FEMA, 2022d). The BCA Toolkit is intended to simplify the BCA by offering predetermined benefits that can be used in place of tailored calculations (FEMA, 2022e)[5] and by automatically applying a discount rate of 7 percent to future benefits (FEMA, 2019a). The BCA Toolkit is a resource to communities that might otherwise have needed to prepare BCAs from scratch or hire consultants to prepare them at considerable cost. Some applicants and subapplicants have expressed interest in having all possible project benefits in the BCA Toolkit precalculated (FEMA, 2020a); however, this runs

---

[4] This is based on an update of projects that had been selected for further review, not a final decision (FEMA, 2021g), although, as noted in Chapter 2, our understanding is that projects that are selected for further review are generally funded. This issue is highlighted in Headwaters Economics (2021a), which notes that 94 percent of all funding was going to East Coast and West Coast states. Headwaters Economics (2021a) highlights eight coastal states (California, the District of Columbia, Maryland, North Carolina, New Jersey, New York, South Carolina, Washington) that account for 90 percent of funding for projects selected for further review.

[5] The availability of precalculated benefit data can greatly simplify the BCA process. For example, if a project's only cost is the acquisition of a property, and that acquisition costs less than the BCA Toolkit's precalculated benefit ($323,000), the applicant can proceed "without the need to complete a full BCA" (FEMA, 2022d, p. 1) because no further evidence is required to prove that the BCR is greater than 1. The process of demonstrating cost-effectiveness is thus simplified, but the cost-effectiveness requirement itself remains.

counter to OMB's desire for more-rigorous, data-backed calculations. Although applicants are not required to use the BCA Toolkit, the vast majority of subapplications are prepared using it.[6]

The values used in the BCA Toolkit are generally national averages for benefits, such as avoided damage for different types of properties. The use of national averages for precalculated benefits provides an implicit advantage to communities where those categories of benefits would have otherwise fallen below the national average. However, projects might help communities or individuals avoid costs that often go uncounted in BCAs—job loss, longer-term housing assistance needs, and other instabilities that might be disproportionately faced by people with lower incomes. In some cases, these instabilities can be difficult to monetize. As discussed in Chapter 5, the BCA Toolkit allows description of nonmonetized benefits, but these descriptions do not count toward the subapplication's BCR.

Some efforts have been made to more flexibly capture benefits that are difficult to monetize. As discussed in Chapter 2, HMGP has adopted the 5 Percent Initiative to support hazard mitigation activities that are difficult to evaluate using FEMA's cost-effectiveness methodologies.[7] This initiative loosens the cost-effectiveness requirement for a limited set of funds and projects, recognizing certain projects with hard-to-quantify benefits might still meet program objectives (FEMA, 2015).

Considerations for Further Incorporating Equity into Hazard Mitigation Assistance Programs' Cost-Effectiveness Assessments

Distributional Weights

Some critics of the HMA grant process argue that current methods to evaluate the distribution of benefits give too much weight to certain benefit components, such as avoided building replacement costs, relative to other potential benefits, such as human health or well-being (Junod et al., 2021). At the heart of these criticisms is a belief that benefits and costs of HMA programs are not distributed optimally among the populations of interest (FEMA, 2020a). Scholars have noted that prevailing BCA methods, such as those commonly used by FEMA and other federal agencies, could be more sensitive to distributional concerns in that they do not explicitly take into account whether project beneficiaries have lower (or higher) incomes or lower (or higher) levels of other welfare-relevant attributes (e.g., disability or minority group status, linguistic isolation) than others in the population (Adler, 2016; McGee, 2021).

Distributional weighting has been discussed since at least the 1950s as a potential avenue to incorporate distributional considerations into policy (Meade, 1955; Scitovsky, 1973). Although distributional weights have not been used in the United States, they are used in Europe. The United Kingdom (UK) *Green Book* contains guidance for inclusion of distributional weights in UK central government program and appraisal evaluation and includes the following definition of *distributional weight*:

> factors that increase the monetary value of benefits or costs that accrue to lower income individuals or households. They are based on the principle that the value of an additional pound of income may be higher for a low-income recipient than a high-income recipient (Her Majesty's Treasury, 2022, p. 54).

---

[6] FEMA staff, conversation with the authors, June 2022.

[7] Activities that might be funded under the 5 Percent Initiative include equipment and systems for warning people of impending hazards; purchase of generators; hazard identification or mapping; acquisition of geographic information system software, hardware, or data to support mitigation; and public awareness or education campaigns.

The economic concept underpinning the rationale for distributional weights in the UK context is the diminishing marginal utility of income (e.g., an additional dollar of income is valued more by someone living below the poverty line than by a millionaire). Some scholars have been critical of the U.S. government for not adopting distributional weights in regulatory or grant programs' BCAs, remarking that distributional weights are derived from a "social welfare function" (SWF) that "defines social welfare as a function of the distribution of utilities in the population" (Fleurbaey and Abi-Rafeh, 2016, p. 286). Some consider standard BCA approaches using Kaldor–Hicks efficiency criteria (Hausman, McPherson, and Satz, 2016) to be inherently normative with implicit weights (Adler, 2011; Arrow, 1951; Farrow, 1998), and they say that alternative weights or SWFs could instead implement decision criteria that achieve different objectives (e.g., distribution of more benefits to disadvantaged households or communities). For example, an SWF could be selected that prioritizes improving the welfare of the worst-off people or maximizing aggregate public safety instead of maximizing aggregate welfare or meeting Kaldor–Hicks efficiency criteria (Adler, 2016; Geistfeld, 2001). Recent critics of the Kaldor–Hicks efficiency criteria assert that, although applying the criteria to BCA might be theoretically elegant, in practice, doing so allows an inequitable distribution of benefits that leaves some affected communities uncompensated (Roman-Romero, 2022). Some might advocate for distributional weights for reasons other than the arguments related to diminishing marginal utility of income: Hazard preparedness, impacts, and recovery have all been shown to differ across socioeconomic factors, such as education or income (Fothergill and Peek, 2004).

In addition to the UK case, the World Bank is an example of an institution that has experience incorporating distributional weights in the form of "social prices" into its BCA methodology. Following heated debate in the 1970s, the practice was formally added to the World Bank's *Operational Manual* in 1980; however, it has been suggested that this practice was "hardly ever used" except in limited experimental cases (Little and Mirrlees, 1991, p. 359). Incorporating distributional weights can be challenging for a variety of reasons, such as lack of consensus about interpersonal comparisons of utility; preferred SWF, weighting schemes, and technical methods; analytical consistency; and data limitations due to the fact that eliciting information about utility and preferences for each member of society affected by a program or policy is prohibitively costly and impractical.

In the case of FEMA's HMA programs, although certain social benefits can be considered in some cases in which the BCR is above 0.75 but below 1, explicit distributional weights are not included in the BCA Toolkit. The incorporation of distributional weights in FEMA HMA programs could expand access to HMA funds by enabling subapplications with BCRs below 1 under current methods to meet the 1 BCR cost-effectiveness requirement, advancing consideration of those subapplications. Additionally, the incorporation of distributional weights could incentivize new subapplications from applicants or subapplicants for which the cost-effectiveness criterion might be more easily met with a distributional weighting scheme.

However, introducing a complex distributional weighting scheme could further burden applicants, thereby discouraging low-resourced applicants that already find the BCA process too difficult to pursue. And adding distributional weights does not address concerns that the types of benefits most relevant to disadvantaged communities might be more difficult to quantify or might not be eligible benefits. A wide variety of distributional weighting schemes exist that could be considered for incorporation into HMA BCA processes toward the goal of reallocating a greater share of grant program benefits to disadvantaged communities. Although these schemes are not the primary focus of this report, Adler (2016) provides a valuable starting point from which to consider this approach to addressing equity concerns in BCA.

Defining Benefiting Areas and Encouraging Subapplications from Disadvantaged Communities

In addition to determining which benefits are considered eligible in a BCA and how those benefits are weighted, determining *who benefits* from a given project is also crucial for BCA outcomes. The Justice40 Initiative states the clear objective that "40 percent of the overall benefits" of certain federal investments, including those made through FEMA's HMA programs, must "flow to disadvantaged communities" (EO 14008). The authors of OMB Memorandum M-21-28, "Interim Implementation Guidance for the Justice40 Initiative," recommended that agencies use existing data on the following indicators of "disadvantaged communities" to implement the goals of the Justice40 Initiative (Young, Mallory, and McCarthy, 2021):

- low income, or high or persistent poverty
- high unemployment and underemployment
- racial and ethnic residential segregation, particularly where the segregation stems from discrimination by government entities
- linguistic isolation
- high housing cost burden and substandard housing
- distressed neighborhoods
- high transportation cost burden or low transportation access
- disproportionate environmental stressor burden and high cumulative impacts
- limited water and sanitation access and affordability
- disproportionate impacts from climate change
- high energy cost burden and low energy access
- jobs lost through the energy transition
- access to health care
- tribal areas.

The OMB guidance also defines *community* as

> either a group of individuals living in geographic proximity to one another, or a geographically dispersed set of individuals (such as migrant workers or Native Americans), where either type of group experiences common conditions. (Young, Mallory, and McCarthy, 2021, p. 2)

The White House Council on Environmental Quality (CEQ) has developed a Climate and Economic Justice Screening Tool (CEJST) in response to EO 14008 to assist federal agencies, including FEMA, in determining which communities might qualify as disadvantaged in support of Justice40 Initiative goals (CEQ, undated). The beta version 0.1 of CEJST indicates whether geographic areas at the census tract level are identified as disadvantaged (CEQ, undated) in the categories outlined above according to CEQ methodology. To be designated as disadvantaged, a census tract must meet CEQ-determined thresholds for one or more environmental indicators and one or more socioeconomic indicators (Scitovsky, 1973). According to CEJST, a census tract can qualify as disadvantaged across one or multiple categories (e.g., workforce development and legacy pollution). It is unclear whether communities designated as disadvantaged across multiple categories receive the same weight as those designated as disadvantaged in a single category. CESJT provides census tract–level data; however, the above OMB definition of *community* also suggests that agencies might have discretion in defining the geographic level of community as more granular (e.g., household level) or more aggregated (e.g., county level). Additionally, the thresholds and benchmarks delineating what makes a community disadvantaged appear to be open to some agency discretion, and such values are known to have crucial implications for policy decisions and successful delivery of 40 percent of HMA programs' benefits to disadvantaged communities (Spielman et al., 2020). According to the data included in the beta version 0.1 of CEJST, 23,470 census tracts (31.7 percent of census tracts in the tool) in the United States qualify as disadvantaged. HMA programs will need to develop clear guidance on (1) how to attribute the flow of benefits from projects that partially benefit disadvantaged communities and partially benefit nondisadvantaged communities and (2) how to accurately assign disadvantaged-community status and benefits to benefiting areas that do not align with county or census tract boundaries.

In contrast to CEJST, FEMA currently uses CDC's SVI to determine disadvantaged status when evaluating HMA program subapplications. According to the FY 2022 notice of funding opportunity (NOFO) for the BRIC program, "areas with SVI greater than or equal to 0.6 . . . are considered disadvantaged" (HMA Division, 2022). According to CDC's publicly available SVI data from 2018, 28,874 census tracts (34.3 percent of those for which data are available) have SVI scores greater than or equal to 0.6 (Agency for Toxic Substances and Disease Registry, 2021). This comparison suggests that the metrics chosen to define *disadvantaged* can significantly influence a community's designated status. Once FEMA has determined and adopted clear definitions of *disadvantaged community*, providing tools similar to CEJST or CDC's SVI map (Agency for Toxic Substances and Disease Registry, 2018) could inform prospective applicants and subapplicants about their disadvantaged-community status and potentially incentivize subapplications from communities to which HMA program benefits are intended to flow as a result of Justice40.

Previous RAND analysis of BRIC subapplication data suggests that applicants and subapplicants often imprecisely specify projects' benefiting areas, with substantial variation in the scope and quality of substantiating documentation provided describing those areas (Finucane et al., forthcoming). Although FEMA requests the name of the county in which the benefiting area is located and that name is unambiguously recorded in BRIC subapplications, project benefits do not always flow along county lines, and, in many cases, benefiting areas were found to be smaller than counties. Because intracounty—or even intraproject—hazard exposure and social vulnerability can vary significantly, improving the precision of subapplication descriptions of benefiting areas can improve accountability by providing FEMA with more-complete and -granular information on project beneficiaries. This information can be used in HMA program evaluation and might help ensure that HMA program benefits demonstrably flow to disadvantaged communities in accordance with Justice40 goals. FEMA could consider providing subapplicants with additional guidance or technical support to increase the precision of subapplications' descriptions of benefiting areas and reduce the burden of preparing precise determinations of project benefit flows and beneficiaries.

Previous HSOAC analysis of FY 2020 and FY 2021 data suggests that BRIC subapplications' imprecise descriptions of benefiting areas make it challenging to accurately determine the percentage of overall benefits of obligated BRIC funds that flowed to disadvantaged communities in those pre-Justice40 program cycles (Finucane et al., forthcoming). Although it is not a perfect analogue, the U.S. Department of Housing and Urban Development's (HUD's) Community Development Block Grant (CDBG) program provides guidance on how to determine an activity's service area (CDBG Program, 2014). Similar detailed guidance might be appropriate for FEMA's HMA programs. Increasing the precision of subapplications' descriptions of benefiting areas and improving attribution of benefit flows could enable more-reliable accounting and evaluation of Justice40 goals.

As discussed in Chapter 2, evidence suggests that many applicants might not be fully documenting project benefits, which we speculate is due to the threshold nature of the BCR requirement. This creates potential challenges for the implementation and evaluation of Justice40 goals. The language of OMB's interim guidance for Justice40 Initiative implementation implies that FEMA must ensure that 40 percent of "overall benefits" from HMA programs are allocated to disadvantaged communities. Regardless of whether the "40 percent of overall benefits" criterion will be applied at the agency, program, or project level, determining whether this goal is being met will be difficult if large portions of project benefits are being systematically left undocumented. On the other hand, increased reporting requirements also represents an increased burden that could deter disadvantaged communities from applying in the first place.

Given the competitive nature of BRIC and FMA and new program parameters for allocation of overall benefits, implementation of Justice40 could incentivize applicants and subapplicants with projects already passing the BCR > 1 criterion to demonstrate additional benefits, particularly benefits flowing to disadvantaged communities. As FEMA develops guidance in response to EO 14008, it might be valuable to consider and anticipate how incumbent applicants and subapplicants will respond to new Justice40-aligned guidance, as well as how implementation might encourage (or not encourage) new applicants and subapplicants, especially those from qualifying disadvantaged communities. FEMA will also need to consider how to faithfully ensure that 40 percent of "overall benefits" flow to disadvantaged communities while recognizing that the cost-effectiveness eligibility criterion does not require an exhaustive nor comprehensive enumeration of project benefits.

Summary of Findings

In this chapter, our analysis of FEMA HMA programs' guidance documents, conversations with FEMA staff and subapplicants, and relevant academic literature produced the following findings:

- Although equity and distributional factors are taken into account during some stages of the evaluation process for BRIC and FMA subapplications in competitive contexts, distributional factors are not explicitly weighted in the BCA process.
- Because states, territories, and federally recognized tribes control which subapplications are submitted to FEMA, they have substantial influence over which subapplications ultimately receive HMA funding.
- Despite considerable efforts by FEMA to ease the burden of conducting BCA to meet HMA programs' cost-effectiveness requirements, particularly through development of the publicly available BCA Toolkit, some applicants and subapplicants still regard the BCA component of the application process as cumbersome.
- Incorporating distributional weights in BCA has been proposed as a potential method for addressing distributional inequities.
- Improving the precision of subapplications' descriptions of benefiting areas and encouraging subapplications from qualifying disadvantaged communities could increase these communities' access to HMA program funds and help meet Justice40 Initiative goals.

CHAPTER 4

Legal, Regulatory, and Policy Issues

An essential component to examining the issues with the equitable access and delivery of mitigation grant benefits is understanding the legal, regulatory, and policy ("the authorities") frameworks under which the grant programs are administered.[1] Therefore, a key task for the HSOAC team was to conduct this examination and analysis and, to the extent practicable, present options to FEMA regarding actions it might consider to address legal, regulatory, and policy impediments to the equitable access and delivery of mitigation grants. To complete this task, we conducted a five-step process to review and analyze the authorities, described in detail in this chapter.

In sum, the HSOAC team found that the relevant authorities applicable to the mitigation grant programs provide FEMA the ability to change, amend, or revise its current policies, processes, and procedures in a manner that the agency determines facilitates greater equitable access and delivery of grants. We found that the applicable authorities do not require FEMA to (1) apply a BCA for applicant eligibility determinations; (2) apply a 7-percent discount rate, as specified in OMB Circular A-94's recommended methodology for BCA, to determine cost-effectiveness; or (3) apply a particular large project notification (LPN) dollar amount (specifically, $1 million) for the purposes of triggering an OMB review process. Notwithstanding these findings, however, we found that the Administrative Procedure Act (APA) (Pub. L. 79-404, 1946) might be triggered in these cases; a prudent option for FEMA would be to take steps so that any changes, amendments, or revisions to current FEMA policies, processes, or procedures are issued consistently with the APA.[2]

---

[1] Pursuant to the requirements of the federally funded research and development center contract between DHS and the RAND Corporation, HSOAC is not authorized to provide the department or its personnel with legal advice, nor may RAND provide legal sufficiency review of department actions, policies, processes, procedures, or the like. HSOAC may provide DHS and its offices and components with only legal research and analysis. The legal research and analysis in this report, therefore, do not constitute legal advice or a legal sufficiency review of FEMA's past, current, or superseding actions, policies, processes, procedures, or similar.

[2] See generally the APA codification at U.S. Code, Title 5, Part I, Chapter 7. The APA applies to all executive branch agencies and "prescribes procedures for agency rulemaking and adjudications, as well as standards for judicial review of final agency actions" (see Garvey, 2017, p. 1). When executive branch agencies "depart from previously established positions by altering or repealing rules or other agency pronouncements [including policy changes]," they generally must provide a "reasoned analysis for the change" (Garvey, 2017, pp. 15–16) (quoting the U.S. Supreme Court case *Motor Vehicle Mfrs. Ass'n*, 1983, at 42–44). Agency actions subject to the APA's requirements include policy statements and guidance documents. See Bowers, 2021, pp. 1–2.

Approach

We used a five-step methodological process to examine and assess these authorities' role and impact on FEMA's administration of the mitigation grant process:

1. Identify the sources of an authority (e.g., Congress, executive branch agency, court).
2. Identify the relevant authority by type (e.g., statute, regulation, EO).
3. Describe the authority (or authoritative document).
4. Review and analyze the authority.
5. Present findings based on the authority.

This approach enabled us to identify, examine, and analyze those authorities that related to the equitable access and delivery of grant funding. We reviewed source documentation and identified substantive elements that addressed the following grant application determination criteria: (1) cost-effectiveness and BCA, (2) discount rate policy (to determine the present value of future costs and benefits described in a grant application), and (3) review and referral of LPNs to OMB.[3] These criteria were identified based on the analysis of grant data, documentary evidence, and the interview information that we collected and examined, as described in Chapters 1 and 2. We found that, when FEMA adjudicates grant applications, these criteria have the most-significant impact on an applicant's ability to gain equitable access to and delivery of federal mitigation grant dollars.

Identifying Sources of Authority

We identified five primary source domains that document authorities related to FEMA's mitigation grant programs:

- congressional legislation (public laws) and reports
- EOs and other executive branch directives, guidance, and policy documents
- judicial and administrative decisions
- academic literature
- other publicly available documents, such as nongovernmental entities' reports and documents, and press reports.[4]

FEMA provided our team with grant mitigation program documentation (e.g., hazard mitigation guidance documentation, grant application documents and tools, FEMA directives, policy memoranda, and standard operating procedures [SOPs]) that referenced these same sources of authorities as being relevant to the execution of the grant programs. Additionally, interviews conducted with FEMA subject-matter experts (SMEs), managers, and staff, as well as with officials and personnel from other federal agencies, provided information that resulted in the identification of these five source domains.

---

[3] We examined the issue of LPNs separately from the issues of the BCA and the discount rate. The LPN is the trigger point at which OMB exercises substantive review of projects to ensure FEMA's adherence to the BCA as a method for determining cost-effectiveness and, therefore, directs FEMA's application of the Stafford Act on this point.

[4] Publicly available source documents were searched using online search engines (e.g., Google, Google Scholar) using the following key words in various combinations: *FEMA, hazard mitigation, grants, application process, notice of funding opportunities, NOFO, cost-effectiveness, benefit-cost analysis, BCA, benefit-cost ratio, BCR, OMB circulars,* and *OMB cost analysis.*

Identifying the Relevant Authority by Type

Once the sources of the authorities were identified, we identified and collected the authoritative documents that addressed or were otherwise applicable to FEMA's management of the mitigation grant programs with respect to issues of equity access and delivery. These included

- federal statutes (i.e., the U.S. Code)
- federal court precedent and binding decisions
- EOs
- federal regulations (i.e., the C.F.R.)
- executive branch policies
- department and agency directives, instructions, and other issuances related to standards and compliance
- department and agency policies, advisory opinions, guidance documents, and SOPs
- other courts' or adjudicative bodies' precedential and nonprecedential decisions
- oversight and review agencies' issuances (e.g., the U.S. Government Accountability Office, offices of inspectors general, the U.S. Department of Justice).

To determine whether a particular documentary source was relevant to the analysis, we qualitatively reviewed and assessed each for whether it addressed (1) cost-effectiveness and BCA, (2) discount rate policy (to determine the present value of future costs and benefits described in a grant application), and (3) review and referral of LPNs to OMB. Additionally, we confirmed the relevance of these documents through interviews with SMEs from FEMA, as well as from other federal agencies.

Description, Review, and Analysis of Authorities

In the next steps of our approach, we reviewed and conducted a qualitative analysis of the relevant authorities in order of their impact on FEMA's ability to manage, amend, and change its hazard mitigation grant programs. Each category has distinct impact on the discretion FEMA will have to change—of its own accord—how it manages the grant programs in a manner that it believes will increase equitable access.

Legal Framework

Like any federal agency, FEMA must comply with public laws and federal statutes and with the federal court decisions that interpret those laws and statutes. To a lesser extent, EOs also fall into this category, but for the fact that EOs cannot violate (or be interpreted or carried out in a manner that would violate) federal laws or statutes. This constitutes the legal framework under which FEMA operates. Any changes to the legal framework must come as a result of congressional enactment, federal court interpretation, or—for EOs—presidential action.

Regulatory Framework

FEMA must also abide by its own published federal regulations and any regulation promulgated by another federal agency with authority or jurisdiction over activities, processes, procedures, or other factors related to FEMA's programs. This constitutes the regulatory framework in which FEMA must abide. Unlike the legal framework, the regulatory framework can be changed by FEMA through the creation, revision, or change of its own published regulations in the C.F.R. and the *Federal Register*. Those regulatory areas over which

FEMA lacks jurisdiction (e.g., budget and accounting, data management) would necessarily be outside of FEMA's ability to alter.

Policy Framework

We group the remaining authorities under the category of policies. These consist of executive branch (presidential or federal department or agency) policies, directives, instructions, memoranda, advisories, guidance documents, SOPs, administrative adjudication decisions, and oversight reports. These authorities constitute the policy framework that affects FEMA to various degrees. Policies are generally not binding on FEMA. FEMA may amend, revise, or change its own policies. The policies of other agencies and entities are merely advisory for FEMA unless otherwise directed by a legal authority. Thus, the policy framework provides FEMA the most leeway in terms of changes it may adopt to increase equitable delivery of mitigation grant resources.

Findings from the Examination and Analysis of Each Category of Authority and Relevant Documents

In this section, we report the results of our qualitative examination and analysis of each category of authority and the relevant documents for each authority.

Legal Framework

The Stafford Act

FEMA's statutory authority for conducting HMA programs is found within the Stafford Act, the landmark legislation passed in 1988 and amended since, governing federal disaster response and recovery activities (Pub. L. 100-707). Under the Stafford Act, FEMA HMA programs are required only to be cost-effective, a requirement that is repeated in the statutory language authorizing these programs.[5] For example, the section of the Stafford Act establishing the BRIC program states that assistance under BRIC may be directed only to "predisaster hazard mitigation measures that are *cost-effective* and are designed to reduce injuries, loss of life, and damage and destruction of property, including damage to critical services and facilities under the jurisdiction of the States or local governments" (U.S. Code, Title 42, Section 5133[b]; emphasis ours). In the section directing how states and local governments may use technical and financial assistance provided under BRIC, the Stafford Act states that assistance may be used "principally to implement predisaster hazard mitigation measures that are cost-effective," among other requirements (U.S. Code, Title 42, Section 5133[e][1][a]). Similarly, the law includes as one of the criteria for awarding assistance under BRIC "the extent to which prioritized, *cost-effective* mitigation activities that produce meaningful and definable outcomes are clearly identified" (U.S. Code, Title 42, Section 5133[g][5]; emphasis ours).

The statutory language in the Stafford Act authorizing HMGP also includes the cost-effectiveness requirement. HMGP provides federal support for hazard mitigation activities in communities after a PD of a disaster (FEMA, 2022f). Through the Stafford Act, HMGP may contribute to

> the cost of hazard mitigation measures which the President has determined are *cost effective* and which substantially reduce the risk of, or increase resilience to, future damage, hardship, loss, or suffering in any

---

[5] See U.S. Code, Title 42, Sections 5133(b), 5133(e)(1)(A), 5133(e)(2), 5133(f)(1), 5133(g)(6), 5133(h)(1), 5133(h)(2), and 5133(j)(3); see also U.S. Code, Title 42, Sections 5170c(a), 5170c(d)(2), and Chapter 68 generally.

area affected by a major disaster, or any area affected by a fire for which assistance was provided under section 5187 of this title. (U.S. Code, Title 42, Section 5170c; emphasis ours)

Although the BRIC program is, by law, focused on mitigation measures that reduce the risk of death, injury, and property damage, HMGP's mandate also extends to reducing the risk of "hardship" and "suffering." HMGP's authorizing statute does not specify a particular methodology for demonstrating that projects are cost-effective and reduce risk. Cost-effectiveness is further mentioned in the context of expediting procedures for providing assistance under HMGP, with the Stafford Act noting that such procedures may include "analysis of the cost-effectiveness and fulfillment of cost-share requirements for proposed hazard mitigation measures" (U.S. Code, Title 42, Section 5170c). Finally, the statutory language authorizing the FMA grant program includes a cost-effectiveness requirement. Specifically, FMA program assistance may be provided only for flood mitigation activities that are "technically feasible and cost-effective" or that reduce disbursements from the National Flood Insurance Fund through acquisition and relocation of flood-prone structures (U.S. Code, Title 42, Section 4104c).

Although the Stafford Act requires FEMA's HMA programs to demonstrate cost-effectiveness, neither *cost-effective* nor any variant of that term is defined in the law. The broadness of this statutorily undefined cost-effectiveness requirement can be contrasted with the more-explicit statutory requirements for other U.S. federal agencies evaluating project costs and benefits. The Water Resources Development Act of 1974 (Pub. L. 93-251, Title I), for example, requires USACE to use a formula published in a designated guidance document to set annual discount rates for calculating the future benefits of projects. This guidance document, originally published in 1962 and titled "Policies, Standards, and Procedures in the Formulation, Evaluation, and Review of Plans for Use and Development of Water and Related Land Resources," adjusts the discount rate in response to variations in the yield of U.S. Treasury securities (Carter and Nesbitt, 2016; U.S. Code, Title 42, Section 1962d-17; U.S. Senate, 1962).

Additionally, no language in the Stafford Act directs FEMA to use a specific discount rate or to use a BCA methodology to demonstrate cost-effectiveness. As a result, we suggest that FEMA may interpret and apply the term *cost-effective* pursuant to its own agency authority. Our justification for this finding is that the U.S. Supreme Court has held in *Chevron U.S.A., Inc. v. NRDC, Inc.*, that deference is given to an agency's interpretation of a statute where that statute is silent or ambiguous with respect to a particular issue, so long as the agency is charged with administering the statute and the interpretation is reasonable.[6] As of September 2022, FEMA had interpreted *cost-effective* to mean that an HMA grant application requires both a BCA and the 7-percent discount rate specified in OMB Circular A-94 for projects; neither the Stafford Act nor *Chevron* or *Skidmore* requires such an interpretation. Our interpretation is that, under both the statute and federal case law, therefore, FEMA may reinterpret *cost-effective* without any of these conditions or with changes to these conditions, so long as they represent a reasonable interpretation of *cost-effective*.[7]

---

[6] See *Chevron*, 1984, at 842–846. Even if a court were to determine that FEMA's grant processes and procedures do not constitute a formal proceeding carrying the force of law that triggers *Chevron* deference (see *United States v. Mead Corp.*, 2001), FEMA would still be entitled to interpret *cost-effective* pursuant to *Skidmore v. Swift*, 323 U.S. 134, 1944 (holding that an agency's interpretation merits some deference given its specialized experience, broader investigation, and information). Because the Stafford Act is silent as to a definition of *cost-effective* or otherwise uses the term in an ambiguous manner, it would be appropriate for FEMA to rely on *Chevron* or *Skidmore* to fashion what it determines to be a reasonable definition in lieu of relying on the Justice40 Initiative and corresponding EOs to do so.

[7] Such a change in interpretation would likely be considered a substantive policy change for FEMA that would likely trigger other requirements under the APA. See the discussion in Chapter 5 in the section titled "Compliance with the Administrative Procedure Act."

Executive Orders: The Justice40 Initiative

In addition to their statutory requirements, FEMA's HMA programs must implement relevant presidential EOs as matter of law. Notably, FEMA is required to implement the president's Justice40 Initiative to ensure that 40 percent of certain federal benefits (including grant assistance) are directed to disadvantaged communities. The Justice40 Initiative was incorporated into EO 14008, "Tackling the Climate Crisis at Home and Abroad," in 2021. In addition, EO 13985, "Advancing Racial Equity and Support for Underserved Communities Through the Federal Government" states that federal agencies should "allocate resources to address the historic failure to invest sufficiently, justly, and equally in underserved communities," in ways that are consistent with relevant law.

Thus, as a legal matter, FEMA is required to interpret *cost-effectiveness* in a manner that is compliant with both the Stafford Act and its own agency regulations (C.F.R., Title 44) *and in a manner that executes the Justice40 Initiative requirements*. Moreover, FEMA's Principle 5 for the BRIC program, aimed at promoting equity, expressly aligns to the Justice40 initiative, stating the goal of "helping members of disadvantaged groups and prioritizing 40 percent of the benefits" for disadvantaged communities (FEMA, 2022b, p. 10807). Therefore, if FEMA determines that the current application of a BCA, the 7-percent discount rate, or the OMB review process (triggered currently by the $1 million LPN) prohibits or otherwise impedes the agency's ability to abide by Justice40 EO requirements,[8] it very likely should reinterpret *cost-effectiveness* so as to abandon or revise these elements in a manner that would better resource underserved communities.

Regulatory Framework

Pursuant to its authority to administer the Stafford Act, FEMA publishes disaster assistance regulations in Title 44 of the C.F.R. These regulations also use, but do not define, the term *cost-effectiveness*. However, HMGP and the FMA program regulations do specify certain elements that may be used to demonstrate cost-effectiveness. The implementing regulation for HMGP is in Part 206 of Title 44 of the C.F.R., titled "Federal Disaster Assistance." Following the Stafford Act requirement that HMGP contribute only to hazard mitigation activities that are cost-effective, the regulation states that projects must "[b]e cost-effective and substantially reduce the risk of future damage, hardship, loss, or suffering resulting from a major disaster" (C.F.R., Title 44, Section 206.434[c][5]).

Although cost-effectiveness is not further described, the regulation does set forth five project elements that grant recipients must demonstrate to meet the HMGP cost-effectiveness and risk reduction requirements. Two of these elements relate to the cost-effectiveness requirement: (1) The recipient must demonstrate that its project "[w]ill not cost more than the anticipated value of the reduction in both direct damages [sic] and subsequent negative impacts to the area if future disasters were to occur" (C.F.R., Title 44, Section 206.434[c][5][ii]), and (2) the recipient must demonstrate that its project "[h]as been determined to be the most practical, effective, and environmentally sound alternative after consideration of a range of options" (C.F.R., Title 44, Section 206.434[c][5][iii]). These regulatory requirements show that FEMA has interpreted *cost-effectiveness* for HMGP to mean that benefits, understood as anticipated reductions in "direct damages" and "subsequent negative impact," must outweigh the costs of a given project. However, the regulation does not prescribe a method or procedure for assessing benefits and costs, nor does it specify which direct and indirect benefits and costs may be considered (and the extent to which they may incorporate economic,

---

[8] OMB has issued guidance on the implementation of the Justice40 Initiative. See Young, Mallory, and McCarthy (2021). Among the guidance within this document are suggestions to consider "program modifications to maximize benefits," including "avoiding potential burdens to disadvantaged communities." See p. 10, Section C.iii. FEMA may leverage this guidance to support an argument that any HMA grant conditions, such as the BCA, the 7-percent discount rate, or any reviewing LPN trigger amount, should be set aside if it constitutes a burden to a disadvantaged community.

social, and environmental concerns) or provide a discount rate or discount rate formula to apply. Additionally, the regulation does not provide an LPN dollar amount triggering review by OMB or any other agency.

Like those governing HMGP, the implementing regulations for the FMA program do not define *cost-effectiveness* (C.F.R., Title 44, Part 77).[9] The FMA regulations do set forth a general cost-effectiveness requirement for the FMA program that is consistent with the Stafford Act language. The regulations state that the purpose of the FMA program is to assist state and local governments in funding cost-effective actions that reduce or eliminate the risk of flood damage to buildings, manufactured homes, and other structures insured under the NFIP (C.F.R., Title 44, Part 77).[10] By focusing on reducing risk to NFIP-insured buildings specifically, FMA projects can help lessen the fiscal impacts of flooding on the NFIP program. In a section on minimum project eligibility criteria, the regulations governing current FMA projects state simply that eligible projects must be cost-effective and reduce the risk of future flood damage (C.F.R., Title 44, Part 77).[11] However, the regulations governing a class of FMA projects with application periods from December 2007 or earlier provide additional guidance about what constitutes cost-effectiveness in a section on minimum project eligibility, largely repeating the language used in the HMGP regulations.

To be considered cost-effective, these projects must not cost more "than the anticipated value of the reduction in both direct damages and subsequent negative impacts to the area if future floods were to occur" (C.F.R., Title 44, Part 77).[12] The regulations go beyond the HMGP regulation by requiring costs and benefits to be "computed on a net present value basis" (C.F.R., Title 44, Part 77).[13] Notwithstanding this and, like with the HMGP implementing regulation, the FMA regulation does not specify which benefits and costs to consider, nor does it require a specific method of determining benefits and costs. It also does not require the use of a particular discount rate or discount rate formula, nor does it impose LPN dollar amount triggering review by OMB or any other agency.

Part 200 of Title 2 of the C.F.R., Uniform Administrative Requirements, Cost Principles, and Audit Requirements for Federal Awards, is a primary source of regulatory guidance for federal agencies on federal grant management policies, procedures, and requirements (C.F.R., Title 2, Part 200). Although this regulation is not specific to HMA programs, it describes the general requirements that all states must meet to be eligible for financial assistance awards.[14] Neither *cost-effective* nor *cost-effectiveness* is defined in this regulation. Subpart E of Part 200 of the C.F.R., Cost Principles, does contain general cost and accounting requirements for entities receiving federal awards (C.F.R., Title 2, Part 200, Subpart E). Subpart E states that a non-federal recipient of a federal award is "responsible for the efficient and effective administration of the Federal award through the application of sound management practices" (C.F.R., Title 2, Part 200, Subpart E). Subpart E further sets forth a series of cost considerations to help determine whether costs are allowable under federal awards. The regulation states that costs must be necessary, reasonable, and allocable to the federal award (C.F.R., Title 2, Part 200, Subpart E).

A reasonable cost is defined as one that "does not exceed that which would be incurred by a prudent person under the circumstances prevailing at the time the decision was made to incur the cost" (C.F.R.,

---

[9] See FEMA (2021d).

[10] See FEMA (2021d).

[11] See FEMA (2021d).

[12] See FEMA (2021d).

[13] See FEMA (2021d).

[14] See OMB et al. (2014), the interim final rule, which became final pursuant to National Archives and Records Administration (2015).

Title 2, Part 200, Subpart E). Allocable costs are those that can be shown to provide benefits in accord with the purpose of the federal award (C.F.R., Title 2, Part 200, Subpart E). Although Part 200 of Title 2 of the C.F.R. contains important regulatory requirements for how FEMA grant recipients may use federal awards, it does not address or dictate how FEMA must interpret *cost-effectiveness* with regard to awarding HMA grants. And, so long as FEMA complies with the general cost principles contained in the regulation with respect to reasonableness, no particular method of BCA, discount rate, or LPN dollar amount is required.

Like with the interpretation of federal statutes, we believe that FEMA may interpret and apply the regulatory term *cost-effective* pursuant to its own agency authority. Our interpretation is based on the following: The U.S. Supreme Court has held in *Auer v. Robbins* that deference is given to an agency's interpretation of its own regulations and rules where the language is ambiguous, so long as the agency's interpretation is not plainly erroneous or inconsistent with the regulation itself.[15] Against this statutory, regulatory, and policy backdrop, FEMA currently interprets *cost-effective* in policy to mean that an HMA grant application requires both BCA and a 7-percent discount rate for projects in excess of $1 million. However, no statute or regulation (not the Stafford Act, the regulations in Title 2 or 44, or *Auer*) requires such an interpretation. Under applicable statutory and regulatory authority (both Titles 2 and 44), therefore, FEMA may amend its policy guidance to redefine *cost-effective* without any of these conditions or with changes to these conditions, so long as the guidance represents a reasonable interpretation of *cost-effective*.[16]

Policy Framework

Our review of the legal and regulatory frameworks governing FEMA's HMA programs shows that FEMA is not directed by the Stafford Act to use a BCA methodology to demonstrate cost-effectiveness, a specific discount rate, or an LPN dollar amount to trigger OMB or other agency review. Moreover, as discussed above, the language of the implementing regulations gives the agency significant latitude to develop its methods and procedures for assessing the benefits and costs of mitigation projects. Our review of relevant FEMA policy documents indicates that, as a policy matter, FEMA has largely adopted OMB Circular A-94's benefit–cost methodology to evaluate the cost-effectiveness of hazard mitigation projects. In particular, FEMA incorporated the benefit–cost methodology set forth in OMB Circular A-94 into its revised HMA guidance in 2015 (FEMA, 2015).

Hazard Mitigation Assistance Guidance

The HMA guidance document provides information and instructions to grant applicants and other stakeholders about FEMA's hazard mitigation programs, including eligibility information and application instructions. In an introductory statement, then–deputy associate administrator for mitigation Roy E. Wright emphasized that the HMA guidance was a significant policy document for FEMA's HMA programs. Wright described the HMA guidance as "the definitive policy document for the Federal Insurance and Mitigation Administration [FIMA]" and expressed his expectation that the document would be "treated as FIMA's offi-

---

[15] See *Auer* (1997, at 457–462). This holding in *Auer* has been narrowed recently by the U.S. Supreme Court in *Kisor* (2019) (holding that the agency's interpretation must be reasonable, be within the agency's authority to make [i.e., it cannot be an ad hoc determination], and fall within the agency's substantive expertise). FEMA appears to meet all the requirements of both *Auer* and *Kisor* with respect to its HMA grant programs, processes, and procedures. And, as with the use of the term in the Stafford Act, the fact that *cost-effective* is not defined in the regulation results in ambiguity as to the particulars of its relevance to a grant application.

[16] Like with our analysis of changes in interpretation of *cost-effective* under Stafford, we note that changing the manner in which FEMA interprets the regulatory version of the term would likely be considered a substantive policy change for FEMA. This would, therefore, likely trigger other requirements under the APA; see the discussion in Chapter 5 in the section titled "Compliance with the Administrative Procedure Act."

cial position on HMA-related matters" (FEMA, 2015). Wright further noted that the HMA guidance identified mitigation strategies by "interpreting the Federal statutes, regulations, and best practices" (FEMA, 2015).

The HMA guidance goes further than the Stafford Act and the HMA implementing regulations by providing a definition of *cost-effectiveness*. This definition explicitly calls for the inclusion of a BCA. In the guidance, cost-effectiveness is defined as being

> [d]etermined by a systematic quantitative method for comparing the costs of alternative means of achiev
> ing the same stream of benefits for a given objective. The benefits in the context of hazard mitigation are
> avoided future damage and losses. *Cost-effectiveness is determined by performing a BCA.* (FEMA, 2015,
> p. 123; emphasis ours)

The guidance also indicates that consistency with OMB Circular A-94 is a FEMA requirement for BCA calculations. Section I ("Cost Effectiveness") of Chapter 4 states that FEMA's BCA software "utilizes the OMB Circular A-94, *Guidelines and Discount Rates for Benefit–Cost Analysis of Federal Programs. FEMA requires the use of approved BCA software (Version 5.0 or greater) to help ensure that calculations are consistent with OMB Circular A-94*" (FEMA, 2015, p. 64; emphasis ours). The guidance generally requires project applicants to achieve a BCR of 1 or more because projects in which "benefits exceed costs are generally considered cost effective" (FEMA, 2015, p. 44).[17] A BCR is defined as a "numerical expression of the cost-effectiveness of a project calculated as the net present value of total project benefits divided by the net present value of total project costs" (FEMA, 2015, p. 122).[18]

Despite this, the guidance does suggest that cost-effectiveness may be demonstrated in other ways, at least under some circumstances:

> FEMA has specified minimum project criteria via regulation (44 CFR Part 79 [now at C.F.R., Title 44,
> Part 77] and 44 CFR Section 206.434), including that Applicants must demonstrate [that] mitigation proj
> ects are cost effective. The determination of cost effectiveness is performed in a variety of ways. It is *typi
> cally* demonstrated by the calculation of a benefit–cost ratio (BCR), dividing total annualized project ben
> efits by total annualized project cost.[19] (FEMA, 2015, p. 44)

However, the guidance limits these occasions by noting that "[o]ther methods to demonstrate cost-effectiveness may be used when they address a non-correctable flaw in the FEMA-approved methodologies or propose a new approach that is unavailable using current tools" (FEMA, 2015, p. 69). FEMA approval is required for alternative BCA methodologies, the guidance notes, although examples of noncorrectable flaws or potential new approaches are not provided.

In addition, the HMA guidance sets forth the submission requirements and eligibility criteria for the 5 Percent Initiative, a HMGP set-aside that allocates as much as 5 percent of HMGP funds for mitigation projects that are "difficult to evaluate using FEMA-approved cost-effectiveness methodologies" (FEMA, 2015,

---

[17] As discussed in Chapter 2, many applicants for hazard mitigation grant funding seek to reach a BCR of 1 without investing additional effort into obtaining the highest possible BCR because higher BCRs do not lead to greater preference in the selection process. This appears to negate some of the value of requiring a BCA to demonstrate cost-effectiveness in that the limited BCAs that applicants perform might not provide a complete picture of the full array of benefits from each project.

[18] It is our understanding that FEMA is referring to "net" benefits as the sum of benefits across the project life cycle rather than the sum of benefits less the sum of costs. The same logic applies to "net" costs. See the "Cost-Effectiveness Assessment in Hazard Mitigation Assistance Programs" section of Chapter 2 for a discussion of how FEMA's BCA software calculates a BCR.

[19] From our conversations with FEMA staff on September 29, 2022, our understanding is that FEMA's use of *annualized* here refers to its BCR calculation software's approach to calculating a BCR, as described in the "Cost-Effectiveness Assessment in Hazard Mitigation Assistance Programs" section of Chapter 2.

p. 111). In its discussion of this initiative, the guidance recognizes that certain mitigation projects might meet the statutory and regulatory cost-effectiveness requirements without conducting a BCA. Projects that are "difficult to evaluate against traditional program cost-effectiveness criteria" but that comply "with Federal, State, and local laws and ordinances" are eligible for the initiative, so long as they meet certain other requirements (FEMA, 2015, p. 112).

Notably, an application under the 5 Percent Initiative may demonstrate project cost-effectiveness through a narrative description only, without conducting a BCA. A narrative description must show that there is a "reasonable expectation that future damage or loss of life or injury will be reduced or prevented by the activity" (FEMA, 2015, p. 112).[20] So although the HMA guidance sets forth the general requirement that a mitigation project applicant demonstrate cost-effectiveness by conducting a BCA aligned with Circular A-94's BCA methodology, the guidance does make exceptions in circumstances in which a BCA would be unsuitable or impractical. Such distinctions speak to the agency's recognition of its own authority to interpret broadly the cost-effectiveness requirements of the Stafford Act and the Title 44 regulations.

Notice of Funding Opportunity

More recently, the NOFO for the FY 2022 BRIC program states, "Applicants and subapplicants applying for hazard mitigation projects must provide a BCA or other documentation that validates cost-effectiveness" (HMA Division, 2022, p. 21). FEMA provides software, the BCA Toolkit, to help applicants calculate their BCRs in a manner that complies with FEMA's standardized methodologies and OMB Circular A-94's requirements (HMA Division, 2022). In particular, the NOFO states that "FEMA has created software to ensure that the BCR is calculated in accordance with FEMA's standardized methodologies and OMB Circular A-94" (FEMA, 2021c, p. 21). However, certain language in the NOFO seems to suggest that methods other than BCA may be used to demonstrate cost-effectiveness as described in Circular A-94. For example, the NOFO states that "applicants and subapplicants applying for mitigation projects must provide a BCA *or other documentation* that validates cost-effectiveness" (HMA Division, 2022, p. 21; emphasis ours) and that a "non-FEMA BCA methodology" may be acceptable "if pre-approved by FEMA in writing" (FEMA, 2021c, p. 21). Moreover, although the NOFO states that all projects must satisfy "applicable cost-effectiveness requirements in compliance with OMB Circular A-94" to be eligible for BRIC funding, it does not expressly state that this requires performing a BCA (HMA Division, 2022, p. 12).

National Advisory Committee Memorandum

Notwithstanding the fact that key FEMA guidance documents appear to reserve some discretion for FEMA to apply a less rigorous cost-effectiveness evaluation to grant applications, the agency has recently reiterated that it considers itself bound to apply the BCA and the 7-percent discount rate specified in Circular A-94. These statements were made in June 2020 in response to recommendations from the NAC. In November 2019, the NAC had presented a report to the FEMA administrator that identified core challenges facing FEMA and offered recommendations for addressing them (NAC, 2019). The NAC report authors argued that the 7-percent discount rate used in FEMA's BCA methodology was "artificially high" because it was based on economic conditions in 1992, when the revised Circular A-94 was issued (NAC, 2019, p. 46). The NAC also argued that "using the artificially high discount rates in the FEMA BCA methodology limits FEMA's ability to approve mitigation projects that are, in fact, cost-effective" (NAC, 2019, p. 45).

To remedy these issues, the NAC recommended that FEMA apply the discount rates in the annually updated Appendix C to Circular A-94. In response to this recommendation and the others contained in the

---

[20] This is not to imply that FEMA does not consider cost along with risk reduction as part of the 5 Percent Initiative. Applicants under the initiative still must demonstrate that the costs of the project are lower than those of competing alternatives.

NAC report, the FEMA administrator at the time, Peter T. Gaynor, provided a memorandum to the NAC chair, W. Nim Kidd, stating FEMA's positions on these topics (Gaynor, 2020). The FEMA memorandum maintained that FEMA lacked the authority to implement the NAC's discount rate recommendation. Echoing the language in Circular A-94 Appendix C, it noted that Appendix C's discount rates may be used only in cost-effectiveness analysis, not in "benefit–cost analysis of public investment."[21] The memorandum does not define *cost-effectiveness* or discuss Circular A-94's description of cost-effectiveness.

FEMA similarly rejected the NAC's recommendation that some BRIC funding be set aside for small projects that would be allowed to demonstrate cost-effectiveness through a narrative description instead of a BCA (NAC, 2019). Such a procedure would mirror the HMGP 5 Percent initiative discussed above. The NAC noted that providing guidance on how projects could apply for BRIC funding without submitting a formal BCA could incentivize new applications. The FEMA memorandum from Administrator Gaynor responded by asserting that the use of BCA to demonstrate cost-effectiveness under BRIC was statutorily required.[22] The memorandum cited the cost-effectiveness requirement in Section 203 of the Stafford Act (codified at U.S. Code, Title 42, Section 5133), which, as discussed above, require mitigation activities under BRIC to be cost-effective but does not define *cost-effectiveness* or mention the BCA technique.

Nevertheless, the memorandum states unequivocally that, for the BRIC program, "FEMA is required to show that projects are cost-effective, *which is demonstrated through benefit–cost analysis*" (Gaynor, 2020, p. 32; emphasis ours). The memorandum notes that FEMA is working to improve "the cost-effectiveness experience" for BRIC applicants, including by working to "streamline the cost-effectiveness process" and to create unspecified new methodologies (Gaynor, 2020, p. 33). Along with the incorporation of FEMA hazard mitigation guidance discussed above, FEMA's position in the NAC response memorandum that demonstrating cost-effectiveness requires a BCA indicates that FEMA would likely need to take administrative actions in accordance with the APA if it decides to revise its policy on how applicants must demonstrate cost-effectiveness.

BCA Training Course

FEMA also states that it is required to conduct BCAs and is bound by the 7-percent discount rate prescribed by OMB Circular A-94 in a FEMA Introduction to Benefit–Cost Analysis training course—an instruction and guidance tool for grant applicants (FEMA, 2022d). The online materials for this course explain BCA concepts and teach course participants how to complete BCAs. In the first unit of the course, the teaching materials pose the question, "Why should I do a BCA?" In reply, it is stated that BCAs are a "required component for HMA projects" (FEMA, 2019a, p. 15). Later in the unit, the teaching materials state that "Federally-funded mitigation projects *must use a discount rate of 7%*, which is set by the U.S. Office of Management and Budget" (FEMA, 2019a, p. 17; emphasis ours). In the teaching materials for unit 3, Circular A-94 is repeatedly cited as governing which costs and benefits are allowable under FEMA's BCA methodology (FEMA, 2019b, pp. 6, 24, 28). For example, the course materials state that, "per OMB Circular A-94, insurance premiums are considered transfer payments and are thus not considered costs (or benefits)" (FEMA, 2019b, p. 28). The inclusion of such statements in official FEMA teaching materials shows that, as a policy matter, FEMA has adopted Circular A-94's BCA methodology and the 7-percent discount rate as part of its process for demonstrating cost-effectiveness, although neither is a required element of cost-effectiveness for FEMA's HMA programs under either the Stafford Act or Title 44 of the C.F.R.

---

[21] As explained in detail in the discussions of the legal and regulatory frameworks, we found that FEMA has the statutory authority to determine cost-effectiveness of HMA grant applications through means other than a BCA.

[22] As explained in detail in the discussions of the legal and regulatory frameworks, we found that FEMA has the statutory authority to determine cost-effectiveness of HMA grant applications through means other than a BCA.

Building Resilient Infrastructure and Communities Federal Register Notice

Most recently, in February 2022, FEMA reiterated its position that it must conform to OMB Circular A-94, suggesting that those who seek a change to the 7-percent discount rate should engage OMB directly. These comments were made in a FEMA notice in the *Federal Register* summarizing its BRIC policy and responding to stakeholder comments about the it (FEMA, 2022b). Several stakeholders had requested that FEMA revisit the 7-percent discount rate requirement for BCA. FEMA responded by citing the statutory cost-effectiveness requirement for the BRIC program: "OMB Circular A-94 applies to Federal programs and sets the requirements for conducting benefit–cost and cost-effectiveness analyses" (FEMA, 2022b, p. 10811). According to FEMA, the agency "cannot revise OMB Circular A-94 and is required to follow it."[23] FEMA advised that "[c]ommenters who believe [that] OMB Circular A-94 is outdated should reach out directly to OMB" (FEMA, 2022b, p. 10811).

Office of Management and Budget Circular A-94

In 1992, OMB issued a revised Circular A-94, titled "Guidelines and Discount Rates for Benefit–Cost Analysis of Federal Programs" (OMB, 1992). The purpose of the revised circular was to assist federal agencies in allocating resources efficiently by providing guidance on sound techniques of economic analysis—notably, BCA and cost-effectiveness analysis. As discussed above, FEMA has largely adopted Circular A-94's BCA methodology to evaluate the cost-effectiveness of hazard mitigation projects. In addition, certain HMA policy and guidance documents and other FEMA materials state or imply that FEMA *must* follow Circular A-94's recommended methodology for BCA, including the use of a 7-percent discount rate, to comply with FEMA's statutory requirement to demonstrate cost-effectiveness.

In this section, we discuss our findings about whether Circular A-94 is, in fact, binding on FEMA. We determined that, as a matter of law and regulation, it is not. We also describe in this section our consideration of whether, even if FEMA is not required to follow Circular A-94, it should use a BCA and a 7-percent discount rate to establish the cost-effectiveness of mitigation projects if it seeks to comply with the circular as a matter of policy. We suggest that FEMA not apply a BCA and a 7-percent discount rate in lieu of our interpretation of the existing legal and regulatory framework.

Is Circular A-94 Binding on FEMA?

As an initial matter, Circular A-94 states explicitly that it is a general guidance document. The circular "provides general guidance [to federal agencies] for conducting benefit–cost and cost-effectiveness analysis" and "specific guidance on discount rates to be used in evaluating Federal programs whose benefits and costs are distributed over time" (OMB, 1992, p. 3). Circular A-94 cites U.S. Code, Title 31, Section 1111, and the Budget and Accounting Act (Pub. L. 67-13, 1921) as its issuance authorities. Neither authority requires federal agencies to be bound to the guidance in Circular A-94 as a matter of law or regulation. As a guidance document, Circular A-94 represents executive branch policy for financial management. More directly, OMB Circular A-94 specifically states that it "does not supersede agency practices which are prescribed by or pursuant to law, Executive Order, or other relevant circulars" (OMB, 1992, p. 3).

Therefore, by its own terms, we do not interpret Circular A-94 as requiring FEMA to apply a BCA, a 7-percent discount rate, or a project dollar amount notification (to OMB) with regard to its HMA programs. This is because, as detailed above, the Stafford Act and the applicable regulations at Title 44 require only that the applications be evaluated based on cost-effectiveness as that term is interpreted by FEMA—the agency Congress has directed to administer the Stafford Act and corresponding regulations. Moreover, the Jus-

---

[23] As explained in detail in the next section, we found that FEMA has the authority to determine cost-effectiveness without applying Circular A-94.

tice40 Initiative EOs require FEMA to apply the cost-effectiveness standard in a manner that shall "allocate resources to address the historic failure to invest sufficiently, justly, and equally in underserved communities," in ways that are consistent with relevant law (EO 13985). Thus, if FEMA determines (as we have found and detailed in this report) that the BCA, the 7-percent discount rate, and the $1 million LPN trigger for OMB review impede FEMA's ability to implement Justice40, FEMA should consider whether it is *legally required* to revise or abandon any of these three conditions.

We interviewed several FEMA personnel about the application of Circular A-94. Interviewees described a view among some FEMA and OMB personnel that OMB had the authority to determine whether and how Circular A-94 applied to the HMA grant programs.[24] Further explanation of this interpretation noted that budget development and execution at executive branch agencies has long been subject to statutory and presidentially directed oversight from OMB and that FEMA's and OMB's statutory authorities must be read together and harmonized. In addition, FEMA staff stated that OMB's statutory budgetary and spending authority requires that notifications to the appropriators be routed through OMB.[25]

Our interpretation is that legal or regulatory authorities do not require this. In fact, the federal courts have found that the operative agency, not OMB, holds the authority to interpret and apply an OMB circular. In *New York v. Shalala*, the District Court for the Southern District of New York—as part of its holding—found that the Secretary of the U.S. Department of Health and Human Services was responsible for interpreting and applying both the governing statutes (i.e., the Social Security Act [U.S. Code, Title 42, Sections 604(a) and 1396b(a)] and OMB Circular A-87) at issue.[26] Therefore, according to our interpretation, whether an HMA grant application requires a BCA or an alternative cost-effectiveness evaluation described within Circular A-94 would be FEMA's determination to make.

This is not to suggest that FEMA, or federal agencies in general, may disregard OMB circulars. In some cases, circulars specifically *direct* federal agencies to take certain actions as a matter of executive branch policy or because the president is using the circular as a vehicle to manage agency processes not otherwise controlled by federal law. For example, Circular A-19 states that agencies "shall incorporate" OMB advice in transmitting their legislative proposals to Congress and "shall not submit to Congress any proposal that OMB has advised is in conflict with the program of the President or has asked the agency to reconsider as a result of the coordination process" (OMB, 1979, Section 8[c][3]). Similarly, Circular A-11 directs agencies to send draft fund control regulations to OMB for approval before posting such regulations on their websites (OMB, 2016, Section 150.7). That said, Circular A-94 has no such directive language, and does not *require*, for example, agencies to use a BCA (as opposed to a cost-effectiveness evaluation) or a 7-percent discount rate with respect to particular grant programs. And, as noted, in the event that an agency and OMB disagree about whether a circular is directive, the operative agency has the authority to interpret the circular's language.[27] If OMB disagrees with the interpretation, it may bring the matter before the Executive Office of the President to be resolved.[28]

Does Circular A-94 Require the Application of a BCA and a 7-Percent Discount Rate as a Matter of Policy?

Circular A-94 by its own terms does not require that FEMA use a BCA and a 7-percent discount rate for the evaluation of HMA grant applications. Circular A-94 clearly states categorically that "*benefit–cost analysis*

---

[24] FEMA staff, interviews with the authors, 2021 and 2022.

[25] FEMA staff, communications with the authors, October 25, 2022.

[26] See *Shalala*, 1997, at 618–622.

[27] See *Shalala*, 1997, at 618–622.

[28] See Farber and O'Connell, 2017.

is recommended as the technique to use in a formal economic analysis of government programs or projects" (Section 5). It further states that "[c]ost-effectiveness analysis . . . can be appropriate when the benefits from competing alternatives are the same or where a policy decision has been made that the benefits must be provided" (Section 5).[29] Circular A-94 defines *BCA* as a "systematic quantitative method of assessing the desirability of government projects or policies when it is important to take a long view of future effects and a broad view of possible side-effects" (OMB, 1992, Appendix A). *Cost-effectiveness analysis*, by contrast, is defined as a "systematic quantitative method for comparing the costs of alternative means of achieving the same stream of benefits or a given objective" (OMB, 1992, Appendix A).

Additionally, Circular A-94 appears to provide significant discretion to FEMA to develop its own BCA and cost-effectiveness methodologies while remaining in compliance with the circular. Circular A-94 says that analyses "should include comprehensive estimates of the expected benefits and costs to *society* based on established definitions and practices for program and policy evaluation" (OMB, 1992, Section 6). Moreover, "[s]ocial net benefits . . . should be the basis for evaluating government programs or policies that have effects on private citizens or other levels of government" (OMB, 1992, Section 6). The guidance goes on to state,

> [s]ocial benefits and costs can differ from private benefits and costs as measured in the marketplace because of imperfections arising from: (i) *external economies or diseconomies* where actions by one party impose benefits or costs on other groups that are not compensated in the market place; (ii) monopoly power that distorts the relationship between marginal costs and market prices; and (iii) taxes or subsidies. (OMB, 1992, Section 6)

In addition, Circular A-94 states, "When benefits and costs have significant distributional effects, these effects should be analyzed and discussed, along with the analysis of net present value" (OMB, 1992, Section 10[a]).

Although Circular A-94 does not specifically define *cost to society* or *social benefit*, Sections 6 and 10 of the circular make clear that not only may FEMA select between applying a BCA or a cost-effectiveness methodology but it may also incorporate social benefits and costs in a manner that it determines is necessary. In light of the president's Justice40 EOs and implementation guidance, the above Circular A-94 language clearly supports FEMA's use of a simpler cost-effectiveness analysis over a BCA, or a BCA that incorporates what FEMA deems to be appropriate social equity factors. Thus, where FEMA is directed by Justice40 Initiative EOs and implementation guidance or where FEMA—as a matter of agency discretion—has made a policy determination that the benefit should be provided, **a cost-effectiveness analysis meets all statutory, regulatory, and policy requirements**.

Circular A-94 recommends that, when one uses the cost-effectiveness analysis approach, a discount rate *based on real Treasury borrowing rates*, rather than a 7-percent base-case analysis rate, be applied for a public investment that might require a BCA (OMB, 1992, Sections 8[b] and 8[c]). Thus, if FEMA determines that a cost-effectiveness analysis is appropriate for certain hazard mitigation grant projects, it may apply a real Treasury borrowing rate for the discount rate. FEMA's current interpretation of Circular A-94 Section 8(b)(1) (i.e., that HMA grants represent a "public investment" requiring the application of a 7-percent discount rate) appears to be a more restrictive interpretation of the framework detailed above (Gaynor, 2020, p. 40). Our analysis suggests that this strict interpretation does not necessarily comport with the statutory and regulatory requirements to apply a cost-effectiveness analysis, which allows for more interpretive leeway regarding discount rates.

---

[29] The phrase "where a policy decision has been made that the benefits must be provided" clearly implies that FEMA may, as a matter of internal agency policy, determine that a program or project should be evaluated using a cost-effectiveness standard rather than a BCA standard.

Additionally, it appears that HMA grant assistance pursuant to the Stafford Act does not constitute simple *public investment* as referenced in Circular A-94 Section 8(b). Section 8 of Circular A-94, "Discount Rate Policy," does not define or describe what constitutes *public investment* for the purposes of advising agencies to apply a BCA in Section 8(b) and the 7-percent discount rated in Section 8(b)(1) (as opposed to a cost-effectiveness analysis in Section 8[c] and Treasury rate–based discount in Section 8[c][1]). Moreover, the Stafford Act does not define or categorize mitigation assistance as a public investment. The statute describes mitigation assistance as "disaster preparedness" designed for the "preparation against disasters, including hazard reduction, avoidance, and mitigation; for assistance to *individuals, businesses, and State and local governments* following such disasters; and for the recovery of damage or destroyed *public* or *private facilities*" (U.S. Code, Title 42, Section 5131[b]; emphasis ours).[30] Thus, the Stafford Act categorizes HMA and related assistance as not only a public investment but an investment that relates to public and *private* security, resilience, recovery, preparedness, and mitigation. Given this, FEMA should consider applying Section 8(c)(1) cost-effectiveness analysis in order to administer the HMA grant program consistently with the Stafford Act, Title 44 regulations, and Justice40 EOs.

Large Project Notifications

As to the issue of LPNs, any triggering dollar amount for projects to be forwarded to OMB review appears to be entirely within FEMA's discretion as a matter of law and policy. The current project cost amount triggering OMB review, $1 million, appears to have been promulgated in a 2012 FEMA recovery SOP (FEMA, 2012, Section 6, especially step 2.6). This dollar trigger amount appears to have also been adopted as part of FEMA's Strategic Funds Management initiative, which was initiated in 2012 (Risk Reduction Division, 2015; see also Carwile, Miller, and Johnson, 2012). FEMA developed this initiative to enhance its management of appropriated DRF monies pursuant to the Budget Control Act of 2011 (Pub. L. 112-25; see Risk Reduction Division, 2015, p. 1). The Budget Control Act of 2011 does not, itself, direct LPN amounts or require that agencies report such amounts to OMB for the purposes of reviewing grant assistance, or any other purpose.

FEMA appears to have determined the $1 million LPN trigger amount as a means for the agency to comply with its requirement to notify Congress of obligations in excess of $1 million pursuant to the annual DHS appropriation bills.[31] This congressional requirement is an accounting notification measure that ensures that all DHS offices, agencies, and components provide Congress with three days' notice before the funds are obligated. It is not a congressional directive to provide a substantive review of how the obligation was determined by the particular DHS office, agency, or component. In other words, in the case of the HMA programs, FEMA is not required to provide information to Congress about how it evaluated the grant application, nor is it required to report that it applies a particular cost methodology, discount rate, or other conditions applicable to the grant adjudication. Additionally, the appropriation act does not require FEMA to submit projects valued in excess of $1 million to OMB for review.[32]

From this information, we found that FEMA must, in accordance with annual DHS appropriation laws, continue to notify Congress within three business days of an obligation in excess of $1 million. However, we

---

[30] See also U.S. Code, Title 42, Sections 5133(c) and 5133(e) (references to "public–private" hazard mitigation).

[31] See the consolidated appropriation acts for FYs 2003 through 2022. For example, Section 507 of Consolidated Appropriations Act, 2022 (Pub. L. 117-103), states, in sum,

> The Secretary of Homeland Security, or the designee of the Secretary, shall notify the Committees on Appropriations of the Senate and the House of Representatives at least 3 full business days in advance of—(1) making or awarding a grant allocation in excess of $1,000,000 . . . .

See also FIMA, 2015, p. 2.

[32] FEMA's decisions about implementing such new policies could have legal implications for the agency that should be further assessed and considered.

also found that FEMA could consider the option of beginning processes to change or amend the dollar trigger amount for notifying OMB or other agencies, so long as the agency does so consistently with the APA and with its internal agency policies and SOPs for making such changes and amendments. It might wish to consult OMB on the implications of such changes. Additionally, we could not find any legal or regulatory prohibition that would prevent FEMA from suspending its practice of notifying OMB of projects in excess of $1 million or inviting substantive OMB review for any HMA program grant awards of more than $1 million should FEMA decide to do so.[33]

Summary of Findings

This chapter presents our analysis of the legal, regulatory, and policy ("the authorities") frameworks under which FEMA administers the HMA grant programs and how those authorities are relevant to the equitable access and delivery of mitigation grant benefits. We conducted a five-step process to qualitatively review and analyze the authorities to determine how current authorities affected FEMA's adjudication of HMA grants with respect to three key issues: (1) use of a BCA for determining applicant eligibility, (2) application of a 7-percent discount rate to determine cost-effectiveness, and (3) use of a particular LPN dollar amount (specifically, $1 million) for the purposes of triggering an OMB review process. This analysis resulted in the following key findings with respect to FEMA's administration of the HMA program:

- FEMA is the federal agency authorized to interpret the meaning of the term *cost-effective* as that term is referenced in the Stafford Act and its implementing regulations at Title 44 of the C.F.R.
- FEMA is authorized to interpret and apply the guidance contained in OMB Circular A-94.
- FEMA is not bound by guidance contained in OMB Circular A-94 if the agency determines that the guidance conflicts or is otherwise inconsistent with the Stafford Act, its implementing regulations at Title 44 of the C.F.R., or any EOs that FEMA is charged to administer.
- FEMA has the discretion to apply either a cost-effectiveness analysis or a BCA to evaluate HMA grant applications so long as the selected method complies with a reasonable interpretation of the term *cost-effective* as that term is referenced in the Stafford Act and its implementing regulations at Title 44 of the C.F.R.
- FEMA has the discretion to apply a discount rate for the evaluation of HMA grant applications based on the U.S. Treasury borrowing rate, a 7-percent discount rate, or any rate in between based those on criteria that the agency reasonably determines.
- FEMA, for the purposes of notification of project funding obligations to OMB or any other federal agency, may apply any dollar trigger amount that it determines to be reasonable.

In sum, we found that FEMA has the authority to change, amend, or revise its current policies, processes, and procedures in a manner that it determines would facilitate more-equitable access and delivery of grants. FEMA may choose to (1) apply a method of analysis other than BCA to establish the cost-effectiveness of grant applications, (2) apply a discount rate at the U.S. Treasury rate up to 7 percent, or (3) select an LPN trigger amount greater than $1 million for the purposes of notification and review by OMB or any outside agency. Notwithstanding these findings, however, we believe that the APA might be triggered, which would call for ensuring that the changes be consistent with the APA, as discussed in Chapter 5.

---

[33] Notification and review are distinct actions. FEMA might elect to notify OMB of its grant obligations as a matter of FEMA policy (perhaps at the same time it notifies Congress). Likewise, the agency might elect to suspend the solicitation of OMB feedback or substantive review of these obligations.

BCA in Other Federal Investment Programs

Project evaluation criteria and methods vary considerably across the federal government. For this portion of the study, we compared the policies, procedures, regulations, and legal requirements of federal agencies that manage discretionary grant programs and infrastructure projects with those of FEMA.

Approach

Specifically, we interviewed program managers across the federal government to identify nonregulatory programs that had BCA requirements. We then reviewed the methodologies used in other programs and compared those with FEMA's BCA process.

To identify potential federal program benchmarks, we reviewed the System for Award Management and NOFOs in the *Federal Register* for discretionary project grants to compile a list of programs. Different federal agencies rely on a variety of statutory authorities and policies for evaluating investments in infrastructure projects. As discussed in Chapter 3, most federal discretionary grant programs operate under the cost principles in C.F.R., Title 2, Subtitle A, Chapter II, Part 200, Subpart E, which states that each project must meet the following criteria:

- **reasonable costs:** The nature of the cost must be ordinary and necessary for the operation of the nonfederal entity or the proper and efficient performance of the federal award, and the amount may not exceed that which would be incurred by a prudent person given the market prices for comparable goods and services for the geographic area at the time of the investment decision.
- **allocable costs:** The cost is incurred specifically for the federal award, benefits both the federal award and other work of the nonfederal entity and can be distributed in proportions that can be approximated using reasonable methods, and is chargeable or assignable to the federal award or cost objective in accordance with relative benefits received.
- **applicable credits:** Receipts that offset or reduce expenses allocable to the federal award as direct or indirect costs (e.g., discounts, rebates or allowances, indemnities on losses, insurance refunds or rebates, and adjustments) received by the nonfederal entity must be credited to the federal award either as a cost reduction or as a cash refund.

For many federal grants, there is no explicit requirement to demonstrate cost-effectiveness. Moreover, very few federal agencies require grant applicants to conduct formal BCAs. Even among those programs that require applicants to demonstrate project cost-effectiveness, some agencies interpret *cost-effectiveness* to mean something other than that the project benefits exceed the costs, such as accomplishing a national objective or providing a specific societal benefit. Thus, for many programs, the necessary and sufficient criteria for applicants include only the following: Ensure that costs are reasonable, demonstrate proper and efficient administration of funds, and comply with the terms and conditions of the federal award.

From our review, we identified the following agencies that use BCA as part of their award processes:

- the Federal Aviation Administration (FAA)
- HUD[1]
- U.S. Department of Transportation (DOT).

And, among agencies that, like FEMA, support water resource planning, we identified the following:

- the Tennessee Valley Authority
- USACE
- the U.S. Department of Agriculture's Natural Resources Conservation Service
- the U.S. Department of the Interior's Bureau of Reclamation.

We found that water resource planning agencies generally followed similar BCA frameworks and used common guidance documents. Therefore, we interviewed officials from only one water resource planning agency. In some cases, we found that federal agencies managed multiple discretionary grant programs; in those cases, we focused on just one or similar programs. For this portion of the study, we interviewed and reviewed policies and regulations for the following programs: (1) USACE's civil works programs, (2) HUD's CDBG programs, (3) DOT's Rebuilding American Infrastructure with Sustainability and Equity (RAISE) discretionary grant program, and (4) FAA's Airport Improvement Program (AIP).

In the rest of this chapter, we document the statutory authority, regulations, guidelines, policies, and procedures related to BCA for these federal programs.

The U.S. Army Corps of Engineers

Background

The formal use of BCA in the evaluation of public investment in infrastructure projects in the United States originated with Public Law 74-738, 1936 (Pearce, 1983). This law, commonly known as the Flood Control Act, authorized civil engineering projects, including water infrastructure and other flood control measures, through USACE and other federal agencies:

> the Federal Government should improve or participate in the improvement of navigable waters or their tributaries, including watersheds thereof, for flood-control purposes if the benefits to whomsoever they may accrue are in the excess of the estimated costs, and if the lives and social security of people are otherwise adversely affected. (Pub. L. 74-738, Section 1)

The Flood Control Act effectively made all federally funded flood control projects subject to a benefit–cost test (Kneese, 1993). However, it made no further mention of net benefits (i.e., benefits minus costs), took a limited view of costs to include only the costs of construction and not any other welfare loss, and did not clearly define what constituted a benefit (Pearce, 1983). Early attempts to develop and formalize economic standards for comparing benefits and costs, including the UK's *Green Book* and OMB Circular A-47, emerged in the 1950s (Committee to Assess the USACE Water Resources Project Planning Procedures, 1999).

---

[1] HUD uses BCA for only specific supplemental appropriations. There is no statutory requirement to demonstrate cost-effectiveness under the Housing and Community Development Act of 1974 (Pub. L. 93-383).

The Water Resources Planning Act of 1965 required the newly created Water Resources Council to establish principles, standards, and procedures for federal water resource planning (Pub. L. 89-80). The 1973 *Principles and Standards for Planning Water and Related Land Resources* (P&S), which developed uniform standards and procedures for evaluating economic benefits and costs of projects, defined the purpose of water and related land resource planning as to promote the quality of life by reflecting society's preference for attaining two national objectives (Water Resources Council, 1973, p. 6):

- To enhance the national economic development by increasing the value of the Nation's output of goods and services and improving national economic efficiency.
- To enhance the quality of the environment by the management, conservation, preservation, creation, restoration, or improvement of the quality of certain natural and cultural resources and ecological systems.

This was the first time national economic development (NED) was explicitly stated as one of the overall purposes of water resource planning (Durden and Fredericks, 2009). The P&S required the beneficial and adverse effects for both of these objectives to be reported in separate "accounts." Additional accounts were established for regional development and social well-being; however, including them in economic studies was not required. This guidance applied to only four agencies: USACE, the Department of the Interior's Bureau of Reclamation, the Tennessee Valley Authority, and the U.S. Department of Agriculture's Soil Conservation Service (later renamed the Natural Resources Conservation Service) (USACE, 2013).

Under the Ronald Reagan administration, the Water Resources Council repealed the P&S and replaced it with the 1983 *Economic and Environmental Principles and Guidelines for Water and Related Land Resources Implementation Studies* (P&G) (Water Resources Council, 1983). This redefined the purpose of water and related land resource planning as solely "to contribute to national economic development consistent[ly] with protecting the Nation's environment, pursuant to national environmental statutes, applicable executive orders, and other Federal planning requirements" (Water Resources Council, 1983, p. iv). The P&G is similar to the P&S in that it also established four accounts—NED, environmental quality, regional economic development, and social well-being—but it required analysis of only the NED objective. Economic analysis of the environmental quality account is typically required by other laws and regulations, such as the National Environmental Policy Act of 1969 (Pub. L. 91-190, 1970).

Over the next two decades, there were many changes in the planning and regulatory landscape, including new environmental considerations and revised cost-sharing rules for water project construction (Committee on Improving Principles and Guidelines for Federal Water Resources Project Planning, 2012). Critics noted that the analytical and planning methods in the P&G were outdated and did not adequately consider uncertainty, nonmarket values, and equity (Panel on Methods and Techniques of Project Analysis, 2004). Congress mandated in Section 2031 of the Water Resources Development Act of 2007 (Pub. L. 110-114) that the P&G be revised to address contemporary planning principles and social and economic priorities, including the following:

- the use of best available economic principles and analytical techniques, including techniques in risk and uncertainty analysis
- the assessment and incorporation of public safety in the formulation of alternatives and recommended plans
- assessment methods that reflect the value of projects for low-income communities and projects that use nonstructural approaches to water resource development and management
- the assessment and evaluation of the interaction of a project with other water resource projects and programs within a region or watershed

- the use of contemporary water resource paradigms, including integrated water resource management and adaptive management
- evaluation methods that ensure that water resource projects are justified by public benefits.

CEQ was tasked with developing the resulting 2013 *Principles and Requirements for Federal Investments in Water Resources* and the supporting 2014 final interagency guidelines (Engineer Research and Development Center, 2014) (together, the PR&G), which were intended to provide a common framework for analyzing an expanded and diverse variety of water resource projects, including other relevant projects, programs, and activities undertaken by the U.S. Environmental Protection Agency, the U.S. Department of Commerce, the U.S. Department of the Interior, the U.S. Department of Agriculture, and DHS (through FEMA) consistently with statutory authorities (USACE, 2013).

Guidance Documents

The civil works programs are still awaiting finalization of agency-specific procedures for the updated PR&G. Although the USACE civil works programs currently rely on the framework in the 1983 P&G, its implementation is based on updated technical assistance from agency directives and planning bulletins. Over the years, USACE has revised its implementation guidance and documented how to interpret the 1983 P&G in Army Engineer Regulation 1105-2-100, also known as the *Planning Guidance Notebook* (USACE, 2000). The *Planning Guidance Notebook* describes the planning process, missions and programs, policies, and analytical requirements under which civil works projects are formulated, evaluated, and selected for implementation (USACE, 2000). Additional Army engineer regulations discuss how risk and uncertainty should be incorporated in economic analyses for, for example, flood risk management studies (USACE, 2000). These requirements ensure that uncertainty is considered and that results are presented in a risk-informed context. Planning bulletins address specific issues in the revised PR&G, such as economic methods to address nonstructural solutions and public safety in feasibility studies (e.g., tolerable-risk guidelines) (USACE, 2019). USACE's Institute for Water Resources also publishes NED manuals, such as the *Economics Primer*, which serve as resource documents for performing economic analyses within USACE's planning framework (Durden and Fredericks, 2009).

BCA Criteria

Under various authorities, most civil works flood risk management projects require BCA.[2] For a typical study, USACE might receive an authorization or appropriation from Congress to consider a specific issue or proposal recommended by a community or state or local government sponsor. Under the Continuing Authorities Program, a flood risk management project with a federal cost share of less than $10 million may be studied and carried out without additional congressional approval.[3] Under the General Investigations Program, a study may be initiated following a request for assistance from a community or state or local government with authorization from Congress. Under the P&G, USACE decisionmakers evaluate projects and make selections based on maximizing net benefits to the country while avoiding environmental issues. Projects are first reviewed by the Office of the Assistant Secretary of the Army for Civil Works and must then be recommended to and approved by Congress.

---

[2] See, for example, Section 206 of the Flood Control Act of 1960 (Pub. L. 86-645, Title II), as amended, and Section 22 of the Water Resources Development Act of 1974 (Pub. L. 93-251, Title I), as amended.

[3] The total cost threshold, which can be up to $15 million, depends on the local cost share, which varies from 35 percent to 50 percent.

Any project with a federal cost share of $10 million or more that meets USACE's evaluation criteria is prioritized based on the BCR and other agency objectives for inclusion in the president's budget request to Congress. Per OMB and agency policy, a USACE project must have a BCR of 2.5 or greater using a 7-percent discount rate to be included in the president's budget request. However, USACE may still recommend projects for congressional authorization if the BCR is below 1 if there is a significant federal interest in the project. Congress ultimately decides whether to authorize and fund a project. Once Congress makes an appropriation, OMB may review projects that will be funded. OMB review is typically limited to project funding decisions involving congressional appropriations and is not required by USACE policies or directives. In some cases, an OMB examiner may request additional information, but OMB does not generally reject projects approved by USACE and Congress for methodological issues in the BCA.[4] OMB review and comment are typically directed at the leadership level to the Office of the Assistant Secretary of the Army for Civil Works, rather than the program level, which is more involved in the evaluation of project BCAs.

Methods

To streamline the BCA process, USACE has developed standardized methods, including uniform methods for calculating benefits, such as standardized depth-damage curves for residential and commercial structures, contents, and vehicles. In recent years, USACE has constructed the National Structure Inventory (NSI), a system of databases containing point-based structure inventories to use in the evaluation of consequences from natural and human-caused hazards.[5] Currently, the primary use of the data is flood damage analysis, but sufficient data exist on each structure to estimate damage due to other types of hazards. One goal of the NSI is to improve U.S. planners' ability to help mitigate future disasters and be usable across all federal agencies. However, in its current form, it might not be sufficient for all agencies to incorporate in their BCAs.

Water projects can have a long useful life. USACE guidance on economic analyses allows a period of analysis that may span 50 or 100 years; this is unlike other discretionary grant programs, which specify that the planning time horizon for certain infrastructure projects should not exceed 20 to 30 years.[6] This allows consideration of longer-term benefits when evaluating projects, particularly when paired with a lower discount rate. USACE guidance also states that appropriate consideration should be given to climate change factors and environmental factors that could extend beyond the period of analysis. USACE guidance specifies that the period of analysis must be the same for each alternative plan considered.

Nonmonetized Benefits and Costs and Other Equity Considerations

To promote equitable outcomes in the distribution of projects, USACE economic analyses generally consider each of the four P&G accounts—not just NED. The additional objectives provide the basis for potential project justifications relying on nonmonetary considerations. Whereas, in the past, BCAs involved calculating only specific categories of economic benefits and costs, USACE studies are now including more-subjective impacts, such as nonmarket values; however, they are not currently doing so in the BCA process. First, USACE methods consider whether a project affects an economically disadvantaged community. A project

---

[4] USACE staff, interview with the authors, 2022.

[5] USACE develop the NSI using data from Hazus, a nationally standardized risk modeling methodology, which is managed by FEMA's Natural Hazards Risk Assessment Program in partnership with other federal agencies, research institutions, and regional planning authorities. Hazus can quantify and map risk information, such as physical damage, economic loss, social impacts, and cost-effectiveness of common mitigation strategies (FEMA, 2022j).

[6] The PUL may be longer than the planning period of analysis, particularly with proper operation, maintenance, repair, replacement, and rehabilitation.

may also be approved using a historical or cultural resource or national significance justification, even if the monetized benefits do not exceed the monetized costs. In addition, projects have been justified by life risk reductions.[7] Ultimately, any project that is not using a purely monetary BCA goes up the chain of command to the Assistant Secretary of the Army for Civil Works for approval.

Discount Rates

The different authorities under which USACE evaluates projects do not necessarily change the overall BCA process; however, in some cases, they might lead to different outcomes because of the use of different discount rates. The Water Resources Development Act of 1974 (Pub. L. 93-251) requires USACE flood risk management projects to use the nominal discount rate for the formulation and evaluation of federal water resource projects rather than the 7-percent discount rate that OMB uses to develop the president's budget, a requirement that commonly causes the projects recommended based on economic analyses to fall below the BCR threshold of 2.5 that is used for the president's budget request (GAO, 2019). Most USACE studies use the federal discount rate for water resource project formulation and evaluation, which is set each FY in accordance with Section 80 of Public Law 93-251 (Bush, 2021). For FY 2022, the water resource planning discount rate was 2.25 percent. For many studies conducted under the Continuing Authorities Program, this is the only discount rate considered. As specified in the agency's economic guidance, for different types of projects, USACE economists may also use different discount rates, including deferred payment interest rates, water supply interest rates, hydropower interest rates, and delinquent payment collection rates, which are also set annually. USACE analysts do not rely on OMB guidance regarding discount rates; however, the agency's technical guidance documents include OMB directives, and they mirror its guidance. As noted above, when the federal cost share is $10 million or greater, a USACE project must have a BCR of 2.5 or greater using a 7-percent discount rate to be included in the president's budget request. However, USACE may still recommend a project that does not meet this threshold if there is a significant federal interest in the project, such as nonmonetary considerations. Local stakeholders may also consider the OMB discount rates in their planning activities.

Summary

USACE's civil works programs have a long history of conducting BCAs for water resource projects that have been increasingly formalized and standardized over time and modernized to achieve more-equitable outcomes. Although USACE currently relies on guidance from the 1983 P&G, numerous more-recent technical documents and revised planning bulletins provide analysts with contemporary BCA techniques for water resource planning. Like other water resource planning agencies, USACE is required by the Water Resources Development Act of 1974 (Pub. L. 93-251) to use specific discount rates, which differ from those recommended by OMB. USACE has developed and continues to develop standardized practices, including new and uniform methods for calculating benefits (e.g., depth-damage curves and contingent valuation studies). To foster the diversity and equitable distribution of projects, USACE approaches have incorporated more subjective criteria, including consideration of nonmarket values. USACE is currently undertaking a comprehensive benefit assessment to expand the use of nonmonetary benefits in its economic analyses.

---

[7] As part of the U.S. Department of Defense (DoD), USACE is not permitted to use monetary estimates of the value of a statistical life in economic analyses.

The U.S. Department of Housing and Urban Development

Background

The CDBG program, authorized under Title I of the Housing and Community Development Act of 1974 (Pub. L. 93-383), provides annual grants on a formula basis to states, cities, and counties to develop viable urban communities. In addition, HUD manages more than a dozen discretionary grant programs. The purpose of CDBG funds is to provide suitable housing, enhance environmental quality, and expand economic opportunities, principally for low- and moderate-income (LMI) people. HUD-related statutes require CDBG-funded activities to meet at least one of three national objectives of the program (CDBG Program, 2014):

- benefiting LMI people
- preventing or eliminating slums or blight
- meeting other community development needs having a particular urgency because existing conditions pose a serious and immediate threat to the health or welfare of the community and other financial resources are not available to meet such needs.

CDBG funds may be used for such activities as the following (HUD, 2022):

- acquisition of real property
- relocation and demolition
- rehabilitation of residential and nonresidential structures
- construction of public facilities and improvements, such as water and sewer facilities, streets, and neighborhood centers, and the conversion of school buildings for eligible purposes
- public services, within certain limits
- activities related to energy conservation and renewable energy resources
- provision of assistance to profit-motivated businesses to carry out economic development and job creation and retention activities.

Activities that fail to meet one or more of the specific tests for meeting a national objective are ineligible. The various statutory authorities for HUD programs generally require project costs to be necessary and reasonable. Thus, CDBG programs do not necessarily require projects to be cost-effective, but they must address a national objective. In this report, we focus specifically on HUD's grants funded through supplemental appropriations for disaster recovery (CDBG-DR), the National Disaster Resilience Competition (CDBG-NDR), and mitigation (CDBG-MIT), each of which has a BCA requirement:

- **CDBG-DR** provides flexible funds to help cities, counties, and states recover from presidentially declared disasters. The primary purpose of CDBG-DR funds is disaster relief, long-term recovery, restoration of infrastructure and housing, and economic revitalization. CDBG-DR funds can also be used to satisfy the nonfederal cost-share requirements of FEMA's Public Assistance program. CDBG-DR is funded by supplemental appropriations for specific disaster-years announced in a *Federal Register* notice. The grantee must submit a disaster recovery action plan to HUD. Projects over a certain cost threshold have a BCA requirement. HUD has wide discretion in the allocation of funds and uses FEMA and U.S. Small Business Administration data to identify the most-impacted and -distressed areas.
- **CDBG-NDR** was announced as a competition in 2014 through a notice of funding availability (NOFA) and operates like the CDBG-DR program with different application rules and requirements. The competition has awarded approximately $1 billion in funding for disaster recovery and long-term community resilience through a two-phase award process. All state and local governments with major disasters

declared in 2011, 2012, and 2013 were eligible to participate in phase 1 of the competition. Following a review of the phase 1 applications, 40 states and communities were invited to compete in the second phase. Each applicant was required to tie its proposals back to the eligible disaster and complete a BCA. On January 21, 2016, HUD announced the 13 CDBG-NDR competition winners.

- **CDBG-MIT** provides eligible grantees opportunities for assistance in areas affected by recent disasters to carry out strategic and high-impact activities to mitigate disaster risks and reduce future losses. Mitigation activities are defined as activities that increase resilience to disasters and reduce or eliminate the long-term risk of loss of life, injury, damage to and loss of property, and suffering and hardship by lessening the impact of future disasters (HUD, undated-a). CDBG-MIT funding availability from supplemental appropriations for specific disaster-years is announced through a *Federal Register* notice. Each grantee must submit a CDBG-MIT action plan that includes a risk-based mitigation needs assessment that identifies and analyzes all significant current and future disaster risks, which provides a substantive basis for the activities proposed. Projects over a certain cost threshold have a BCA requirement.

Guidance Documents

A NOFO or NOFA is published each year on Grants.gov for HUD's annually appropriated funds and standing programs. For funds administered as a result of special supplemental appropriations, HUD communicates to grantees and the general public primarily by *Federal Register* notice. For CDBG-NDR, which awarded funds on a competitive basis, NOFOs and NOFAs described the type of funding available and provided information on submitting applications, as well as specific guidelines for conducting BCAs. HUD also added an appendix to its competition instructions with basic guidance to conduct a BCA and use add-on values for environmental quality and social cohesion benefits, which can be challenging to quantify (HUD, 2015). The applicant is asked to provide up to three pages of narrative if it cannot qualify based on the quantified benefits and costs alone.

The various supplemental CDBG programs state that grantees may use existing local, state, or federal BCA methodologies considered to be the most appropriate to account for the full range of physical, economic, social, and environmental costs and benefits, so long as HUD determines the approach to be acceptable for this purpose. As an additional resource, HUD refers grantees to other agencies' BCA technical guidance documents, such as FEMA's *Ecosystem Service Benefits in Benefit–Cost Analysis for FEMA's Mitigation Programs Policy* (Deputy Associate Administrator for Insurance and Mitigation, 2020) or DOT's "Treatment of the Value of Preventing Fatalities and Injuries in Preparing Economic Analyses" (DOT, 2021a). Additional BCA trainings prepared by HUD staff and partner federal agencies, such as FEMA, are available for grantees on HUD Exchange, an online platform for providing program information, guidance, services, and tools to HUD's community partners (HUD, undated-b).

BCA Criteria

There is no formal requirement to conduct a BCA for the CDBG program, except for (1) cost-share and (2) underwriting projects. For CDBG-DR and CDBG-MIT, there is a BCA requirement for covered projects. A covered project is a large-scale infrastructure project having a total project cost of $100 million or more (with at least $50 million in CDBG funds) that is an activity or group of related activities that develop physical assets designed to provide or support services to the general public in any of the following sectors:

- aviation
- surface transportation, including roadways, bridges, railroads, and transit
- ports, including navigational channels

- water resource projects
- energy production and generation, including from fossil, renewable, nuclear, and hydro sources
- electricity transmission
- broadband
- pipelines
- stormwater and sewer infrastructure
- drinking water infrastructure.

In addition, each finalist that advanced to the second phase of the CDBG-NDR competition was asked to prepare a BCA. For CDBG-DR and CDBG-MIT, covered projects must demonstrate long-term efficacy and fiscal sustainability and demonstrably benefit a most-impacted and -distressed area. This involves documenting measurable outcomes or risk reduction and having a BCR equal to or greater than 1. Despite these requirements, typically few covered projects exceed $100 million each year. One principal reason is that applicants often undertake incremental investments in resilience rather than very large infrastructure projects. Therefore, typical grants are much smaller than $100 million. It is unclear whether grantees are designing projects to avoid triggering additional requirements by exceeding this threshold. However, HUD has typically seen grantees making incremental investments in resilience over a period of years, the sum of which are intended to have significant regional mitigation impacts.

Methods

Most HUD funds are available and allocated through block grants without a formal BCA process. Furthermore, BCA does not serve as the sole determinant as to whether covered projects requiring $50 million or more in CDBG funds will be funded. HUD analysts described a built-in social return-on-investment framework that first considers whether activities meet any of three statutory national objectives.[8] The grantee must also demonstrate, upon completion of the project, that it met the national objective. HUD recognizes that formal BCA could skew awards away from areas HUD is statutorily required to address. HUD staff noted that, when analysts are evaluating resilience to natural disasters, BCA tends to favor protecting higher-value properties in wealthier communities, while one of HUD's national objectives is to benefit LMI people and households. HUD is concerned that existing methods tend to undervalue benefits related to property, contents, and—in particular—environmental quality and social cohesion in LMI neighborhoods and areas where grantees propose to use CDBG funds. Thus, HUD sets a high project cost threshold for covered projects to require a BCA.

HUD does not rely on a single BCA methodology but provides flexibility based on the nature of the project. Specifically, grantees may use any appropriate existing local, state, or federal BCA methodologies that HUD determines to be acceptable. HUD strongly encourages grantees to use the FEMA BCA Toolkit or any existing BCA that has been accepted by USACE, DOT, or FEMA. HUD collaborates with other federal agency SMEs in providing guidance on the BCA methodologies prior to submission. Although a grantee maintains the discretion to use a BCA methodology or approach best suited to the project, every acceptable methodology and approach must include certain baseline elements or considerations to create an underlying degree of uniform comparison and consistency with OMB Circular A-94. HUD allows each BCA team to choose an appropriate period of analysis given the nature of the project; that planning period may exceed 50 years, particularly if one of the project goals is to provide environmental benefits. Table 5.1 shows types of allowable benefits in one of HUD's BCA frameworks.

---

[8] HUD staff, interview with the authors, April 2022.

TABLE 5.1

Allowable Benefits in the Community Development Block Grant National Disaster Resilience Competition

Type of Benefits	Description
Resilience	Reduction of expected property damage due to future or repeat disasters
	Reduction of expected casualties from future or repeat disasters
	Value of reduced displacement caused by future or repeat disasters
	Reduced vulnerability of energy and water infrastructure to large-scale outages
Environmental	Ecosystem and biodiversity effects
	Reduced energy use
	Noise levels
	Reduced greenhouse gas emissions
	Reduced criterion pollutants
	Reduced stormwater runoff
	Reduced urban heat-island effect
Social	Reductions in human suffering (e.g., lives lost or illness from exposure to environmental contamination)
	Benefit to LMI people or households
	Improved living environment (e.g., elimination of slum and blight conditions, social cohesion, improved recreational value, greater access to cultural and historical sites and landscapes)
	Greater housing affordability
Economic revitalization	Direct effects on local or regional economy (e.g., tourism revenue) net of opportunity costs
	Value of property other than through enhanced flood protection

SOURCE: HUD, 2015.

Nonmonetized Benefits and Costs and Other Equity Considerations

HUD has determined that, for the majority of projects, allowable activities must meet one of three statutory national objectives and, with the exception of covered projects requiring more than $50 million in CDBG funds, do not require a formal BCA. Thus, fewer projects are subject to the BCA requirement, which could pose a potential cost barrier for investments in LMI and disadvantaged communities. Furthermore, for any project that requires a BCA, HUD provides a degree of flexibility in allowing any BCA or methodology approved by USACE, DOT, or FEMA—which can provide additional resources and expertise to help monetize hard-to-quantify benefits—and allowing qualitative descriptions of benefits to be considered as evidence, as appropriate, within the BCA. Both the high cost threshold for a formal BCA and the flexibility to consider additional types of monetized or nonmonetized benefits might mitigate equity concerns about who ultimately receives grants and ensures that projects in disadvantaged communities are not unduly disqualified.

Discount Rates

HUD generally requires grantees to follow BCA guidance in OMB Circular A-94. For example, HUD directs applicants to use the base-case discount rate in OMB Circular A-94 of 7 percent when calculating the net present value of a project. OMB's general principles for BCA or cost-effectiveness analysis also direct analysts to include an evaluation of alternatives to achieve program objectives by different means (OMB, 1992). HUD interprets OMB's guidelines on the evaluation of alternatives to allow the use of different discount rates for CDBG-funded activities. Therefore, CDBG programs with BCA requirements provide additional flexibility in choosing discount rates for evaluating projects if grantees use a discount rate of 3 percent or higher and provide justification acceptable to HUD based on the nature of the proposal.

HUD has noted several reasons that OMB guidance is incompatible with evaluating CDBG activities. First, HUD's statutory mission to accomplish national objectives is inconsistent with OMB's BCA guidance. As noted above, BCA tends to favor protecting higher-value properties, while one of HUD's national objectives is to benefit LMI people and households. Furthermore, there is concern that the use of higher discount rates can mathematically discourage investment in projects with high up-front costs and long-term benefits in favor of projects with short-term benefits or those in which costs are distributed over a longer time horizon. Some types of projects seeking CDBG funds (e.g., green infrastructure) are expected to provide benefits over a long time horizon, perhaps 50 to 100 years. The nature of future discounting means that the present value of benefits that accrue further into the future are more sensitive to the discount rate being used to assess cost-effectiveness. For example, after 50 years, the discounted monetized value of an annual benefit calculated using a 7-percent discount rate would be less than 4 percent of the monetized value of the benefit if it were realized in year 1 (or as calculated on an undiscounted basis).[9] The same benefit received in year 50 calculated using a 3-percent discount rate would have a monetized value equivalent to approximately 24 percent of the monetized value if it were realized in year 1. This does not imply that future discounting is inappropriate, and discount rates should not be adjusted in order to alter perceptions of whether a project is truly cost-effective.

Second, HUD considers factors, including social considerations, that favor less heavily discounting future benefits when "citizen participation" in the disaster recovery and resilience planning process suggests that there is a strongly held community preference for alternatives that provide long-term benefits in favor of short-term benefits. HUD's mandate for "citizen participation" in the CDBG program, authorized under Section 104(a)(2) of the Housing and Community Development Act and by regulations at C.F.R., Title 24, Section 570.486(a)(6), might help reveal community preferences in how local stakeholders value future benefits. For example, challenges in the wake of disasters (e.g., community relocation) might require complex decisions with more to consider in terms of alternatives and how to weight future benefits and costs. In such cases, HUD might allow an applicant to use a lower discount rate in its BCA.

Third, public investment could displace private consumption rather than private investment. For some CDBG projects, a 7-percent discount rate might be appropriate because CDBG-funded activities could displace private investment in housing, community development, and economic revitalization. However, OMB has stated that, when activities displace private consumption (e.g., through higher consumer prices for goods and services), a lower discount rate is appropriate (OMB Circular A-4). The nature of the private activity being displaced matters, and HUD has noted the importance of calculations using discount rates below 7 percent when private consumption is more heavily affected than investment and the grantee provides supporting justification.

---

[9] This is calculated as

$$\sum_{t=1}^{T} \frac{B_t}{(1 + r)^{(t-t_1)}}$$

where t is the number of years after the investment (t_1 is the year of the initial investment), B_t is the monetized benefit in year t, and r is the real discount rate.

Thus, HUD allows the use of alternative discount rates that comport with HUD's mission, capture environmental and social benefits that might accrue over a longer time horizon, or better reflect the anticipated impacts of the activity. HUD directs grantees to use OMB's recommended 7 percent as the base-case discount rate but allows and reserves the right to authorize projects that use alternative discount rates. HUD also allows grantees to use any BCA that has been approved by USACE, which also uses alternative discount rates. In these ways, CDBG programs have attempted to harmonize OMB guidance with HUD's national objectives. According to HUD staff, OMB does not raise objections to HUD decisions solely to critique HUD's use of alternative discount rates.[10]

Summary

Statute does not require HUD programs to be cost-effective, but every activity must meet at least one of three national objectives. However, several HUD programs funded through disaster supplemental appropriations mandate a formal BCA for any covered project having a total project cost of $100 million or more (with at least $50 million in CDBG funds). This relatively high cost threshold addresses some equity concerns about who receives grants and helps ensure that projects with benefits that are hard to quantify, particularly those in disadvantaged communities, are not unduly disqualified. Furthermore, HUD recognizes that some benefits (and costs) might be difficult or impossible to quantify and allows qualitative descriptions to be considered and weighted, as appropriate.

HUD provides a great deal of flexibility in terms of its approach in allowing grantees to use any appropriate existing local, state, or federal BCA methodologies that the agency determines to be acceptable. Specifically, HUD will allow any existing BCA that has already been accepted by USACE, DOT, or FEMA. HUD generally requires grantees to follow BCA guidance in OMB Circular A-94 but provides discretion in selecting discount rates for evaluating projects if a grantee uses a discount rate of 3 percent or higher and provides justification acceptable to HUD based on the nature of the proposal.

The U.S. Department of Transportation

Background

In 1966, Congress established DOT to develop "national transportation policies and programs conducive to the provision of fast, safe, efficient, and convenient transportation at the lowest cost consistent therewith and with other national objectives, including the efficient utilization and conservation of the Nation's resources" (Pub. L. 89-670, Section 2[a]). In response to the Great Recession that occurred between 2007 and 2009, Congress passed a stimulus package, the American Recovery and Reinvestment Act of 2009 (Pub. L. 111-5), providing supplemental appropriations for job preservation and creation, infrastructure investment, energy efficiency and science, unemployment assistance, and state and local government fiscal aid. The act created the Transportation Investment Generating Economic Recovery (TIGER) discretionary grant program for DOT to invest in road, rail, transit, and port projects that promised to achieve crucial national objectives. Funds would be awarded on a competitive basis for projects that would have significant impact on the United States, a metropolitan area, or a region.

Consolidated Appropriations Act, 2021 (Pub. L. 116-260, 2020), included $1 billion for National Infrastructure Investments, rebranded as RAISE discretionary grants. FY 2021 funds were awarded to a total of 90 projects (63 capital projects and 27 planning projects) in 47 states. The RAISE grant program, previously

---

[10] HUD staff, interview with the authors, April 2022.

TIGER and Better Utilizing Investments to Leverage Development (BUILD), has awarded 13 rounds of competitive grants totaling nearly $10 billion for National Infrastructure Investments through the FY 2021 appropriation process. Since 2009, the program has funded 769 projects in all 50 states, the District of Columbia, Puerto Rico, Guam, and the U.S. Virgin Islands (Office of Operations, 2022).

The Infrastructure Investment and Jobs Act (Pub. L. 117-58, 2021), also known as the Bipartisan Infrastructure Law, authorized and appropriated $1.5 billion in FY 2022 to be awarded under the RAISE grant program. Additional funding was made available under Consolidated Appropriations Act, 2022 (Pub. L. 117-103). At least $35 million of the total funding is guaranteed to go toward projects located in areas of persistent poverty (APPs) or historically disadvantaged communities (HDCs). Consolidated Appropriations Act, 2021, defines a project as being in an APP for the RAISE grant program if any of the following three conditions is true:

- The county in which the project is located had consistently greater than or equal to 20 percent of the population living in poverty in all three of the following datasets:
  - the 1990 decennial census
  - the 2000 decennial census
  - the 2020 Small Area Income and Poverty Estimates.
- The census tract in which the project is located has a poverty rate of at least 20 percent as measured by the 2014–2018 five-year data series available from the American Community Survey of the U.S. Census Bureau.
- The project is located in any territory or possession of the United States.

The 2022 NOFO for the RAISE grant program, consistent with OMB's interim guidance for the Justice40 Initiative, defines a project as being in an HDC if any of the following three conditions is true (Office of Operations, 2022):

- The project is in a qualifying census tract.
- The project is on tribal land.
- The project is in any territory or possession of the United States.

Under the Infrastructure Investment and Jobs Act (Pub. L. 117-58, 2021), the RAISE program expanded the number of communities eligible for 100-percent federal share of funding—specifically, those in rural communities, APPs, and HDCs. To advance DOT's goal to award projects in APPs and HDCs, the agency created an APP and HDC Status Tool, released on January 28, 2022, to help an applicant determine whether its project location meets one of these definitions.[11] The mapping tool uses information from the U.S. Census Bureau and other sources to identify these areas. Examples of eligible RAISE projects include the following (Office of the Under Secretary for Policy, 2022):

- highway, bridge, or other road project
- public transportation projects
- passenger and freight rail projects
- port infrastructure investments (including inland port infrastructure and land ports of entry)
- surface transportation components of an airport project eligible for assistance in the AIP
- intermodal projects

---

[11] As of July 18, 2022, the tool was available at DOT, undated.

- projects to replace or rehabilitate a culvert or prevent stormwater runoff for the purpose of improving habitat for aquatic species
- transportation facilities on tribal land
- planning and preconstruction activities for any of the above.

Guidance Documents

The principal guidance document for applicants to DOT's discretionary grant programs is the *Benefit–Cost Analysis Guidance for Discretionary Grant Programs* (Office of the Secretary, 2022). DOT's BCA guidance is revised each year to remain consistent with new and amended instructions in NOFOs published in the *Federal Register*. The most-recent guidance was released in March 2022. Recent updates have included new methodologies for estimating the benefits of improved pedestrian, cycling, and transit facilities and the health benefits of active transportation; new categories of benefits, including stormwater runoff and wildlife impacts; and updated parameter values (Office of the Secretary, 2022, p. 5). Updates to the guidance prepared by DOT staff are commonly based on literature reviews, research on topics that is incorporated into standard BCA practices, and methods in past (successful) applications that were generally applicable to other projects, well-researched, and carefully documented.

DOT's BCA guidance provides an overview of the BCA framework, general principles for BCA, approaches to assessing some of the most-common types of benefits, requirements for presenting costs (or cost savings), and methods for comparing benefits and costs (i.e., net benefits and BCR). The guidance emphasizes that DOT's review process and evaluation methodology are consistent with EO 12893 and OMB Circular A-94. In addition to NOFOs and DOT's BCA guidance, workshops and webinars are provided for potential applicants to specific discretionary grant programs on the preparation of a BCA during the application window for each program.[12] DOT staff economists also provide technical assistance to applicants through the final application deadline for each discretionary grant program. Applicants may also request project debriefs after the BCA review process.

BCA Criteria

There is no statutory requirement for the RAISE grant program to conduct project BCAs. Nonetheless, at the onset, DOT made the policy decision to require certain applicants to complete formal BCAs. Initially, the TIGER grant program had tiered requirements: An applicant requesting less than $20 million in federal funding was not required to submit a BCA; an applicant requesting between $20 million and $100 million in federal funding was required to include a basic BCA; and an applicant requesting more than $100 million in federal funding was required to submit a more comprehensive BCA (GAO, 2011). Around 2015, DOT eliminated this tiering and required every TIGER applicant for a capital project to submit a BCA. This reflects the agency's general opinion that cost-effectiveness "should be demonstrated rather than assumed."[13] BCA has since become formally integrated into the agency's discretionary grant review process. Statutory requirements have subsequently been established for other DOT discretionary grant programs to use BCA. For example, the Federal Highway Administration's Nationally Significant Freight and Highway Projects program, which provides competitive Fostering Advancements in Shipping and Transportation for the Long-Term Achievement of National Efficiencies (FASTLANE) grants for nationally and regionally significant

---

[12] See, for example, DOT, 2021b.

[13] DOT staff, interview with the authors, 2022.

freight and highway projects, must consider "the cost effectiveness of the proposed project" (U.S. Code, Title 23, Section 117[e][3][A]) in addition to the project's impact on "mobility in the State and region in which the project is carried out" (U.S. Code, Title 23, Section 117[e][3][B]) and "safety on freight corridors with significant hazards" (U.S. Code, Title 23, Section 117[e][3][C]). Currently, about nine or ten DOT programs require BCAs; only certain programs have statutory requirements. Occasionally, to prioritize other national objectives, Congress writes appropriation bills in a manner that exempts transportation projects in certain programs (e.g., investments at small U.S. ports or projects outside the contiguous United States) from the BCA requirement.

In the RAISE grant program, the minimum award for capital projects and planning projects is $1 million in rural areas and $5 million in urban areas. Although there is no exemption for smaller capital projects, a planning project that does not involve construction is not required to conduct a BCA. However, because the minimum award is relatively large, it is less likely that many potential applicants are declining to submit smaller capital projects because they believe that the cost of preparing a BCA would exceed the anticipated benefits of the project. In the past, DOT analysts would prepare BCAs for applicants that could not complete their own. Today, DOT analysts still review project BCAs and may contribute additional benefit calculations using approved methods if the applicant on its own could not quantify certain types of standard benefits that comparable projects typically include. These program features suggest that, to improve equitable access to awards, DOT has taken steps to mitigate the potential cost barrier of preparing a BCA.

The RAISE grant program uses a two-step application review process because of the large number (i.e., more than 100) of applications received each year. First, DOT evaluates safety, environmental sustainability, quality of life, mobility and community connectivity, economic competitiveness and opportunity, state of good repair, partnership and collaboration, and innovation as merit criteria (Office of Operations, 2022). DOT staff assign a rating—the ratings consider whether the benefits are clear, direct, and significant, thus yielding a rating of high, medium, low, or nonresponsive—for each merit criterion, and those ratings are then used to calculate an overall merit rating to determine which projects will advance in the competition. The safety, environmental sustainability, quality of life, and mobility and community connectivity merit criteria are weighted more heavily in the process to advance projects for further analysis. Note that some of the merit criteria, such as safety, also factor directly into the BCA. According to the merit criterion ratings, each project is designated an overall rating as follows:

- Highly Recommended if six or more of the eight merit criteria ratings are "high" and none of the merit criteria ratings are "non-responsive."
- Recommended if at least one, but no more than five, of the merit criteria ratings are "high", no more than three of the merit criteria ratings are "low", and none are "nonresponsive."
- Acceptable if there is a combination of "high," "medium," "low," or "non-responsive" ratings that do not fit within the definitions of Highly Recommended, Recommended, or Unacceptable.
- Unacceptable if there are three or more "non-responsive" ratings. (Office of the Secretary, 2023, p. 39)

Highly recommended projects automatically advance, and recommended projects are reviewed to identify projects with significant merits to advance for further analysis. Capital projects that advance are subject to a more in-depth review in the second phase and are evaluated based on specific BCA criteria. For the BCA review, DOT assigns each project to one of four BCR ranges (less than 1.0, 1.0 to 1.5, 1.5 to 3.0, or above 3.0) and a confidence rating (high, medium, or low) for the assessment. DOT has stated that a project with a BCR of less than 1 "will not be selected for an award, unless the project has unquantified benefits that demonstrate clear outcomes for underserved communities" (Office of the Secretary, 2023, pp. 56–57). Projects are typically reviewed by a staff economist, a secondary senior staff member, the chief economist who assigns a recommended rating, and a senior review team that evaluates projects for all DOT programs, before the project proceeds to review by the Secretary of Transportation. Generally, OMB does not review project BCAs for the RAISE grant program. OMB plays a role when DOT publishes NOFOs and in the development of evaluation criteria but otherwise has no formal role in DOT's BCA process.

Methods

To streamline and simplify the BCA process, DOT has, over time, introduced more-formal guidance that did not exist when the TIGER grant program began—starting with instructions on general BCA methods and technical guidance for calculating certain types of benefits and eventually combining these documents into the BCA guidance—and offered additional annual training webinars for applicants. DOT's BCA guidance provides a standardized methodological framework for preparing BCAs for discretionary grant applications, reference materials for key inputs and assumptions, recommended precalculated benefits and costs, and sample calculations for some of the quantitative elements of a BCA (Office of the Secretary, 2022). Specific reference materials cited in the BCA guidance, such as DOT's "Treatment of the Value of Preventing Fatalities and Injuries in Preparing Economic Analyses" (DOT, 2021a), are also used more broadly by the agency and other federal agencies in regulatory analyses and other economic studies.

Appendix A of DOT's BCA guidance provides recommended parameter values for various types of benefits and costs that DOT recommends that applicants use in their BCAs, including monetized values and other key inputs. Applicants are also permitted to include additional categories of benefits and costs and values different from those recommended by DOT, but they must provide documentation of sources, detailed calculations of monetized values, and their rationale for using alternative values. Table 5.2 reports the types of benefits and sources included in DOT's BCA guidance.

DOT has noted that it considers uncertainty about the future (e.g., how travel markets and patterns might shift or evolve over time) a limitation on the usefulness of modeling project benefits over a long time horizon because those estimates might be less reliable. Therefore, DOT has recommended that applicants avoid using a period of analysis exceeding 30 years. However, in *Benefit–Cost Analysis Guidance for Discretionary Grant Programs*, DOT recommends that, when project assets have a useful lifetime greater than this time horizon (e.g., road and rail bridges, tunnels, or other major structures), the applicant include an assessment of the value of the remaining asset life (Office of the Secretary, 2022). The BCA guidance provides a relatively simple methodology and example calculation for estimating the residual value of an asset.

Nonmonetized Benefits and Costs and Other Equity Considerations

DOT has recommended that applicants include a qualitative discussion when certain benefits and costs cannot be easily or reliably monetized, and the department weights these nonmonetized elements in the BCA review process. DOT has recognized that incorporating nonmonetized benefits in the evaluation process requires subjective judgment, but, in a situation in which the project falls just below the BCR threshold and nonquantified benefits are likely to be realized, DOT considers this additional factor for grant eligibility (and award). As noted above, a project with a BCR of less than 1 will not be selected for an award unless the project demonstrates clear, unquantified outcomes consistent with one of two merit criteria: environmental sustainability and quality of life.

DOT has recommended that, as an additional equity consideration, applicants use national average values to calculate certain benefits. Specifically, regardless of differences in income levels that might reflect significant existing disparities, applicants can use standardized values for travel time savings and fatalities and injuries avoided. Therefore, lower-income communities are not disadvantaged when calculating identical benefits to wealthier communities. However, this does not entirely remove perceived biases in BCA methods that incorporate an economic baseline that bakes in existing disparities in socioeconomic conditions and

TABLE 5.2

Recommended Parameter Values in the U.S. Department of Transportation's BCA Guidance

Type of Benefit	Unit of Measurement	Reference
Value of reduced fatalities and injuries	Per crash	Table A-1
Property damage–only crashes	Per vehicle	Table A-2
Value of travel time savings	Hourly by activity, purpose, and operator type	Table A-3
Average vehicle occupancy rates for highway passenger vehicles	Per vehicle (by travel time, peak vs. off-peak)	Table A-4
Vehicle operating costs	Per mile (by vehicle type)	Table A-5
Damage costs for emissions per metric ton	Per metric ton	Table A-6
Inflation adjustment values	Multiplier to adjust to real 2020 dollars	Table A-7
Pedestrian facility improvements revealed preference values	Per use; per person-mile walked	Table A-8
Cycling facility improvement revealed preference values	Per cycling mile	Table A-9
Transit facility amenity revealed and stated preference values	Per user trip (by amenity)	Table A-10
Transit vehicle amenity values	Per user trip (by amenity)	Table A-11
Mortality reduction benefits of induced active transportation values	Per induced trip	Table A-12
External highway use costs: noise and congestion values	Per vehicle-mile traveled	Table A-13

SOURCE: Office of the Secretary, 2022.

environmental justice. Furthermore, DOT does not use federal share as a selection criterion in awarding projects.

In discussions with our team, DOT staff did not recommend incorporating additional distributional analysis into the BCA process or using distributional weights because doing so would considerably increase the amount of information requested from applicants.[14] DOT has indicated, as have other federal agencies, that, if a distributional analysis is required for equity considerations, it is best conducted separately from the BCA.

Discount Rates

DOT requires applicants to use a real discount rate of 7 percent, which is consistent with OMB Circular A-94. Previously, the TIGER grant program required applicants to report findings using real discount rates of both 3 percent and 7 percent—both discount rates are required for regulatory analyses as described in Circular A-4—however, this practice was eliminated for DOT's discretionary grant programs. The one exception to this rule is estimating the benefits of reductions in greenhouse gas (GHG) emissions—specifically, carbon dioxide (CO_2) emissions. DOT stated that, "because GHG emissions can have long-lasting, even intergenerational impacts, unlike all other categories of benefits (including reductions in other emissions) and costs, benefits from reductions in CO_2 emissions should be discounted at a 3 percent rate" (Office of the Secretary,

---

[14] DOT staff, interview with the authors, July 19, 2022.

2022, p. 18). DOT has noted that this policy is consistent with OMB guidance on longer-term benefits (Office of the Secretary, 2022, p. 50).

Summary

Since passage of the 2009 American Recovery and Reinvestment Act, additional congressional bills and supplemental appropriations have authorized DOT to award discretionary grants on a competitive basis for infrastructure investment in road, rail, transit, and port projects that promise to achieve crucial national objectives. Although there is no statutory requirement for the RAISE grant program to conduct project BCAs, DOT policy requires all applicants to prepare BCAs for capital projects. Since 2009, other DOT discretionary grant programs have implemented formal or statutory requirements for project BCAs. And since its inception, the RAISE (formerly TIGER and Better Utilizing Investments to Leverage Development [BUILD]) grant program has developed BCA principles, framework, and methods that have been formally incorporated into the DOT's BCA guidance, which is revised each year to reflect new instructions in NOFOs and developments in acceptable methods, including estimating the value of different types of benefits and costs. DOT recommends that an applicant include a qualitative discussion when certain benefits and costs cannot be easily or reliably monetized, and it weights these nonmonetized elements in the BCA review process. Although projects that have BCRs below 1 will generally not be selected for an award, those projects that demonstrate clear, unquantified outcomes—particularly those that meet specific merit criteria—may remain eligible and ultimately succeed. DOT requires applicants to use a real discount rate of 7 percent in project BCAs, which is consistent with OMB Circular A-94.

The Federal Aviation Administration

Background

After the end of World War II, the Federal-Aid Airport Program was authorized by the Federal Airport Act of 1946 (Pub. L. 79-377) with funding from the general fund of the U.S. Treasury to provide grants to state and local governments to help develop a system of airports to meet the country's needs (FAA, 2017). The program's grants could be used for construction of airfields, passenger terminals, and access roads and to purchase land for airport development. Grants were often used to support converting military airports for civilian use but, by the late 1960s, proved to be insufficient to address growing capacity needs at U.S. airports (Tang, 2019).

In 1970, more-comprehensive options were established, with grants for airport planning under the Planning Grant Program and for airport development under the Airport Development Aid Program authorized by the Airport and Airway Development Act of 1970 (Pub. L. 91-258). These programs were funded by a newly established Airport and Airway Trust Fund, which collected revenues from user fees on airline fares, air freight, and aviation fuel. The authority for these grant programs expired in 1981.

The successor grant program, AIP, was authorized by the Airport and Airway Improvement Act of 1982 (Pub. L. 97-248, Title V). AIP provides aid under a single program for airport planning and development and is authorized under U.S. Code, Title 49, Section 48103, to draw on funds from the Airport and Airway Trust Fund. Periodic FAA reauthorization acts and other public laws have amended and extended the AIP several times. The first amendment, enacted just one month after the initial law was passed, authorized FAA to convert unused apportioned funds for use in the award of discretionary grants (Pub. L. 97-276, 1982). Most recently, the AIP was extended through FY 2023 under the FAA Reauthorization Act of 2018 (Pub. L. 115-254).

The AIP provides grants to public agencies and, in some cases, private entities for planning and development projects at public-use airports that align with prescribed federal priorities in the National Plan of Integrated Airport Systems. U.S. Code, Title 49, Section 47101, lists the policy directives and aviation priorities of the United States:

- Provide a safe and secure airport and airway system.
- Minimize the effect that airport noise has on nearby communities.
- Develop reliever airports, cargo hub airports, and intermodalism.
- Protect natural resources.
- Reduce aircraft delays.
- Convert former military air bases to civil use or improving joint-use airports.
- Carry out various other projects to ensure a safe and efficient airport system.

Once authorization and appropriation are in place, the approved AIP funding is split into defined categories and types according to formulas in the FAA Reauthorization Act (e.g., based on enplanements or volume of cargo processed). Similar to HMA being composed of multiple grant programs, the AIP has several fund categories and approximately 12 different funding programs, each of which has distinct formulas and set-aside requirements for determining how funds are distributed. Table 5.3 shows examples of eligible and ineligible AIP projects.

Guidance Documents

FAA Order 5100-38D, referred to as the AIP handbook, provides guidance to FAA staff about administration of the AIP (FAA, 2019). The AIP handbook provides an overview of the application process. The handbook contains, among other key program information, specific eligibility criteria for entities that eligible to apply for AIP grant funding and for projects. An AIP grant recipient, referred to as a sponsor, can be a public agency owning or leasing a public-use airport to an entity that does not currently own an airport (e.g., a municipal planning agency).

In addition to the AIP handbook, the FAA Office of Aviation Policy and Plans published *FAA Airport Benefit–Cost Analysis Guidance*, which provides detailed instruction to airport sponsors on conducting BCAs for capacity-related airport projects (Office of Aviation Policy and Plans, 2020). Capacity projects are defined in FAA Order 5090.5 as

> the minimum development or equipment that is required to reduce delay or improve an airport or system of airports for the primary purpose of maintaining access or accommodating more passengers, cargo, aircraft operations, or based aircraft, or allow access to a broader fleet mix. (Planning and Environmental Division, 2019, p. A-2)

The BCA requirement does not apply "to projects undertaken solely, or principally, for the objectives of safety, security, conformance with FAA standards, or environmental mitigation" (Office of Aviation Policy and Plans, 2020, p. 1) The FAA BCA guidance lists the required components of a BCA, including definition of project objectives, specified assumptions, identification of base-case and reasonable alternatives, evaluation (and quantification) of benefits and costs, comparison of alternatives, sensitivity analysis, and recommendations. BCA principles from OMB Circular A-94 (e.g., using a base-case discount rate of 7 percent and inflation projections from the president's budget and excluding labor and output multiplier benefits) are largely incorporated in FAA's BCA guidelines.

TABLE 5.3

Examples of Eligible and Ineligible Airport Improvement Program Projects

Eligibility	Example Project
Eligible	Construct or rehabilitate a runway, taxiway, or apron.
	Install lighting, signage, or drainage for an airfield.
	Acquire land.
	Construct a weather observation station.
	Develop a navigational aid.
	Conduct a planning or environmental study.
	Improve a safety area.
	Develop a plan for airport layout.
	Build an access road that traverses only airport property.
	Remove, lower, move, mark, or light a hazard.
	Purchase a glycol recovery or vacuum truck to be owned and operated by the airport.
Ineligible	Purchase maintenance equipment or vehicle, an office or office equipment, or artwork.
	Construct a fuel farm or aircraft hangar.[a]
	Landscape.
	Develop an industrial park.
	Develop a marketing plan.
	Perform training.
	Make an improvement for a commercial enterprise.
	Maintain or repair a building.

SOURCE: FAA, 2021.

[a] This type of project might be conditionally eligible at a nonprimary airport. For more information, see Miller et al., 2020.

FAA also relies on a document entitled *Economic Values for FAA Investment and Regulatory Decisions, A Guide,* which includes updated and standardized economic values for use in FAA investment and regulatory decisions, including the AIP grant-making process (GRA, 2007). This guidance was issued as a result of the work of FAA's Aviation Rulemaking Cost Committee, which was established by FAA Order 1110.132 in 2002 (FAA, 2002). The objective of the guidance is to encourage uniformity across investment and regulatory analyses for reliable comparison. Within this guidance document, economic values fall into three general categories: (1) passenger-related values (e.g., value of passenger time); (2) aircraft-related values (e.g., aircraft operating and ownership costs); and (3) aircraft restoration and replacement costs. FAA has recommended that sponsors use the economic values in this guidance document for BCAs in the AIP application process (GRA, 2007).

BCA Criteria

The primary focus of the AIP is airport development and planning projects. AIP funds are typically first apportioned into major entitlement categories, such as primary, cargo, and general aviation. Remaining funds are distributed to a discretionary fund. Eligible projects include those improvements related to enhancing airport capacity, safety, security, and environmental concerns. Previously, any airport capacity project with a cost of $5 million or more in AIP discretionary grant funding was required to conduct a BCA (FAA, 1999). This cost threshold was subsequently increased. FAA's BCA guidance currently states that "airport capacity projects meeting a dollar threshold of $10 million or more in AIP discretionary grants over the life of the project and all airport capacity projects requesting LOIs [letters of intent] must be shown to have total discounted benefits that exceed total discounted costs" (Office of Aviation Policy and Plans, 2020, p. 1). Projects for reconstruction or rehabilitation of critical airfield structures may be exempt from BCA requirements on a case-by-case basis (Office of Aviation Policy and Plans, 2020).

The sponsor is required to conduct a BCA to demonstrate that project benefits exceed their costs or that the BCR is equal to or greater than 1. FAA staff noted that the BCR is one criterion but not the sole determinant of a successful AIP grant application. It is possible for a project with a BCR of less than 1 to be awarded AIP discretionary funds because of FAA's consideration of other hard-to-quantify benefit and impact categories not captured by the BCA process (e.g., macroeconomic impacts or benefits to the wider aviation network) (Office of Aviation Policy and Plans, 2020).

Methods

Prior to 1997, FAA analysts conducted a BCA for each capacity project seeking significant discretionary funding, although the process lacked any formal standardization. In 1997, FAA changed this policy, and sponsors were required to complete more-standardized BCA with assistance from FAA (FAA, 1997). Sponsors typically use aviation planning consultants but also draw on assistance from FAA field offices and work the chief economist in FAA's Office of Aviation Policy and Plans in the final phase of BCA development. A BCA is required only for capacity-related projects costing $10 million or more in AIP discretionary funds. The majority of applications are for projects with funding amounts below this threshold;[15] in 2022, only eight of 47 funded projects exceeded that threshold (FAA, 2022). FAA has noted that a full-fledged BCA covering a wide variety of alternatives can take one or more years to complete and involve advanced modeling, depending on the complexity, magnitude, and technical requirements of the project.[16] Given the potential cost barrier to meeting the BCA requirement, FAA guidance highlights factors sponsors should consider when determining the "appropriate level of effort" to put into a BCA. The guidance also recommends that sponsors communicate with FAA in advance of preparing a formal BCA to ensure that the level of effort is likely to produce a BCA that meets FAA standards (Office of Aviation Policy and Plans, 2020, p. 29).

Generally, the benefits of capacity-related airport improvement projects accrue to current and future airport users primarily as cost savings associated with reduced travel time or time spent within the airport system. Other potential benefits include the ability to accommodate larger (longer-range) aircraft, noise mitigation, reduced aircraft emissions, and compliance with FAA standards for airport safety, security, and design. A description of potential benefits from capacity-related airport improvements are listed in FAA's BCA guidance, as are recommended approaches to calculating benefits and references to specific economic models. FAA's BCA guidance also describes widely used evaluation criteria and calculations that may be presented in the BCA to provide economic justification for the potential investment, such as net present value, BCR, and internal rate of return. The sponsor must also choose an appropriate time horizon for the study. FAA guidance defines three appropriate evaluation periods for consideration: (1) requirement life, (2) physical life, and (3) economic life. FAA has stated that the requirement life should not exceed 30 years and typically recommends a period of 20 years following completion of construction as the project's useful

---

[15] FAA staff, interview with the authors, June 21, 2022.

[16] FAA staff, interview with the authors, June 21, 2022.

economic life (Office of Aviation Policy and Plans, 2020). FAA guidance states that, "to the extent that physical life exceeds economic life, it is, by definition, not an appropriate time period" (Office of Aviation Policy and Plans, 2020, p. 26).

Nonmonetized Benefits and Costs and Other Equity Considerations

FAA's BCA guidance encourages sponsors to include qualitatively described or nonmonetized (i.e., hard-to-quantify) benefits and other benefits not formally incorporated into BCA in AIP grant applications. FAA directs sponsors to provide "if possible, a range in which a dollar value could be reasonably expected to fall should be reported" (Office of Aviation Policy and Plans, 2020, p. 9). FAA guidance also states that hard-to-quantify benefits and costs "should not be neglected and can be very important to the outcome of the analysis" (Office of Aviation Policy and Plans, 2020, p. 9). FAA guidance provides recommended approaches (e.g., delay propagation multipliers, contingent valuation studies) for three common types of hard-to-quantify benefits:

- measurement of systemwide delay caused by local airport delay
- passenger comfort and convenience
- nonaviation macroeconomic and productivity impacts.

Although they are not included in the BCA, these hard-to-quantify benefits and costs may still be weighted in the AIP grant decisionmaking processes. Specifically, consideration of these hard-to-quantify benefits can influence which project alternatives sponsors recommend in the AIP applications and can also make a project application with a BCR of less than 1 allowable. FAA staff have stated that the agency does not make project funding determinations based on a single metric (i.e., the BCR) and that hard-to-quantify benefits are an additional consideration that meaningfully factors into allocative decisionmaking.[17]

Regarding equity, the FAA's BCA guidance notes that one step in the BCA process is to "perform distributional assessment when warranted," suggesting that distributional assessment may be included in AIP BCA but is not universally required. The guidance document does not describe the conditions under which distributional assessment in BCA is warranted.

Incentives to participate in the AIP, including alternative sources of airport funding and the time to prepare a BCA, vary by airport size. Smaller airports are less likely than larger airports to experience capacity constraints or delays but may request funds for runway extensions to accommodate larger aircraft, for example. FAA staff noted that the $10 million project cost threshold for capacity-related AIP discretionary funding may *increase* equity and access in that applications from smaller airports or for smaller projects are not burdened by the BCA requirement.

Discount Rates

FAA generally relies on the prescribed real discount rate of 7 percent and practices in OMB's guidance in OMB Circular A-94. The FAA Office of Aviation Policy and Plans also recommends that discount rates of 4 percent and 10 percent be used in addition to the base-case discount rate of 7 percent in sensitivity analyses (Office of Aviation Policy and Plans, 2020, p. 89). Alternative discount rates may be used with justification; however, FAA generally avoids approaches that are inconsistent with OMB guidance.

---

[17] FAA staff, interview with the authors, June 21, 2022.

Summary

The broad goals of the FAA AIP are airport development and planning to improve safety and efficiency of airport and aviation operations. Although most AIP funds are apportioned to airports by formulas as entitlements, a portion of remaining AIP funds are allocated to a discretionary fund and awarded on a competitive basis. Only a relatively small portion of applications for AIP discretionary grant funds require a formal BCA. Specifically, any capacity-related project requiring $10 million or more in AIP discretionary funds or requesting a letter of intent requires a BCA—therefore, smaller airports and projects can generally submit applications without BCA. This contrasts with FEMA's HMA program, which places the burden of preparing a BCA on a broader variety of applicants, including those submitting smaller, lower-cost projects.

Generally, FAA's BCA guidance aligns with principles from OMB Circular A-94. However, as is the case with other federal agencies' investment and regulatory decisionmaking criteria, the BCR is not the single determinant of an AIP project application's success. Such factors as sector-specific hard-to-quantify benefits (e.g., macroeconomic impacts and quality-of-life considerations) are weighted in conjunction with standard BCA results. In addition, the results of sensitivity analyses using alternative discount rates are considered. In interviews, FAA staff noted that the majority of applications they receive each year do not require BCA because they are below the $10 million project cost threshold. FAA staff stated in interviews that it is possible that the $10 million cost threshold triggering a BCA requirement could be increasing access and equity among sponsors seeking discretionary AIP funds, relative to a lower threshold, because smaller airports and projects are not burdened with the costs of preparing full-fledged BCA along with their applications to establish eligibility and competitiveness.[18]

Benchmarking FEMA BCA Policies, Procedures, and Requirements to Those of Other Agencies

Although many agencies rely on similar guidance for project evaluation, such as OMB Circular A-94 and the P&G for water resource planning, their individual policies and practices vary in notable ways. Table 5.4 summarizes benchmarks for BCA policies, procedures, and requirements for each of the agencies and programs we analyzed in comparison to FEMA. Overall, the key areas in which other agencies' BCA practices differ from FEMA's are

- a project cost threshold below which activities do not require a formal BCA
- additional categories of allowable benefits (e.g., quality-of-life improvements, economic or labor market opportunities, value of time savings)
- qualitative (or nonmonetized) benefits considered in program eligibility and project evaluation and award selection
- use of different discount rates in evaluating alternative means of achieving program objectives (particularly with regard to environmental or social benefits) or as required by law (e.g., water resource planning)
- BCR being one of multiple eligibility criteria; in some cases, agencies use entirely different merit-based criteria to determine eligibility (e.g., achieving a national objective)
- BCR factoring directly into award selection criteria along with other factors, such as a confidence rating for the assessment
- no formal notification to OMB and generally limited interaction with OMB examiners.

---

[18] FAA staff, interview with the authors, June 21, 2022.

TABLE 5.4
Comparison of FEMA BCA Policies, Procedures, and Requirements with Those of Other Agencies

Criterion	Agency and Program				
	FEMA	FAA AIP	DOT RAISE	HUD CDBG-DR, CDBG-NDRC, and CDBG-MIT	USACE
Project requires a BCA	All projects, with few exceptions (e.g., 5 Percent Initiative)	Capacity-related airport projects requiring more than $10 million in AIP funds	All projects; awards start at $1 million in rural areas and $5 million in urban areas	Covered projects with a cost of $100 million or more (with at least $50 million in CDBG funds); CDBG-NDRC applicants	All projects; additional congressional approval required for any project with a federal cost share of $10 million or more
Guidance documents	*BCA Reference Guide* (FEMA, 2009); *Supplement to the Benefit–Cost Analysis Reference Guide* (FEMA, 2011); *Hazard Mitigation Assistance Guidance: Hazard Mitigation Grant Program, Pre-Disaster Mitigation Program, and Flood Mitigation Assistance Program* (FEMA, 2015)	FAA Order 5100.38D; *FAA Airport Benefit–Cost Analysis Guidance* (Office of Aviation Policy and Plans, 2020); supporting documents	*Benefit–Cost Analysis Guidance for Discretionary Grant Programs* (Office of the Secretary, 2022); NOFO; BCA webinars	NOFO or NOFA with BCA instructions (periodically); BCA technical documents	P&G (1983) and supporting documents
Methodology	BCA Toolkit; guidance provides standardized methodology and precalculated benefits.	Guidance provides standardized methodology.	Guidance provides standardized methodology.	Any BCA approved by USACE, DOT, or FEMA; or any acceptable local, state, or federal BCA methods.	Guidance provides standardized methodology and precalculated benefits (e.g., damage curves).
Consideration of nonmonetized benefits or costs	BCA Toolkit allows description of nonmonetized benefits, which does not count toward BCR.	Nonmonetized benefits may be considered in evaluating alternatives.	Nonmonetized benefits may be considered in evaluating alternatives.	Alternative demonstration of benefits for LMI and vulnerable populations if BCR < 1.	Nonmonetized benefits considered; may count toward eligibility if BCR < 1.
Specified time horizon	May exceed 50 years	Minimum PUL specified in guidance (varies, up to 40 years)	PUL (not to exceed 30 years)	May exceed 50 years	May exceed 50 years
Specified discount rate	7%	7% base case; alternative discount rates allowed with justification	7%	7% base case; alternative discount rates allowed with justification	Discount rate for water resource planning set annually, by law (FY 2022: 2.25%)
Eligibility	BCR ≥ 1	BCR ≥ 1 or qualitative criteria, such as how the project fits into the wider national airport network	BCR ≥ 1 or merit criteria (e.g., safety, environmental sustainability, quality of life)	Meet one of three statutory national objectives	BCR ≥ 2.5 at 7% discount rate for projects ≥$15 million or approval of Assistant Secretary

Tables 5.5 and 5.6 show the different types of benefits included in each agency's BCA guidance documents. As shown in the tables, the types of benefits allowed for consideration in BCAs vary across federal programs because of the nature of the projects. In some cases, the inclusion of specific types of benefits is allowable in an agency's BCA framework only if a certain BCR threshold has already been met.

These differences across agencies could create some inconsistency in terms of where federal dollars are allowed to be spent to achieve different types of benefits, depending on the funding agency. Specifically, such benefits as quality-of-life improvements, economic or labor market opportunities, value of time savings, and reduced emissions or energy costs are permitted to be counted in only certain programs and contexts. In contrast, HUD's process allows grantees to use any BCA that has been approved by USACE, DOT, or FEMA. Although this differential treatment of federal dollars might be efficient if agencies have differing abilities to access particular types of benefits or if policy preferences dictate that funds focus on specific uses, these limitations on benefit categories could also limit an applicant's ability to surpass BCR thresholds even if the project were desirable from a federalwide perspective. An agency might have primary benefits targeted by its mission, but co-benefits may also be considered contemporaneously.

Interviewees from several agencies noted concerns about the reliability of monetized values for certain types of benefits (e.g., social or recreational impacts) or benefits calculated over a very long time horizon because of uncertainty about the future. Analysts were generally concerned about false precision in the benefits and costs presented in BCA (i.e., higher confidence in the accuracy of those estimates than justified by the data). As a potential remedy, in the review process, some agencies, including DOT and HUD, assign a confidence rating (e.g., high, medium, low) to the benefits and costs calculated in the BCA that factors into the award process.

Summary of Findings

This chapter presents a comparison of the policies, procedures, regulations, and legal requirements of federal agencies that manage discretionary grant programs and infrastructure projects. We spoke with program managers across the federal government to identify discretionary grant programs and other nonregulatory programs that had BCA requirements. We then reviewed the methodologies used in other programs and compared those with FEMA's BCA process.

We found several areas in which FEMA's methodology differed significantly from those of other federal agencies:

- First, most agencies require only projects that exceed a certain cost threshold to conduct formal BCA. Thus, fewer projects are subject to the BCA requirement, which could pose a cost barrier for investments in disadvantaged communities.
- Second, other agencies consider a wider variety of potential benefits in the BCA—including nonmonetized benefits (e.g., social cohesion, quality-of-life improvements)—which might help some applicants with hard-to-quantify benefits achieve a higher BCR to meet the minimum evaluation criteria and perform more favorably against other projects in award selection.
- Third, some (not all) agencies provide flexibility in choosing discount rates other than the 7-percent real discount rate in OMB's guidance. This changes the BCR or net present value calculation for projects, particularly those for which costs and benefits do not occur at the same point in time.
- Fourth, although most agencies consider the BCR in determining program eligibility, most also consider other factors, such as achieving a national objective or providing an agency-desired benefit, and do not necessarily disqualify every project with a BCR less than 1 if there are other compelling federal interests. In most programs, unlike FEMA's, the BCR factors directly into the award selection crite-

TABLE 5.5
Social and Economic Benefits Included in Various Federal Agency BCA Guidance Documents

Benefit	Agency and Program						Metric
	FEMA	FAA AIP	DOT RAISE	HUD CDBG-DR or CDBG-NDRC	HUD CDBG-MIT	USACE	
Social and economic							
Increase safety.	x	x	x	x	x	x	Injuries, deaths
Increase security.		x			x		Injuries, deaths
Improve user quality of life (e.g., accessibility, comfort, convenience, health benefits, community impacts).		x	x	x	x	x	Various (qualitative)
Reduce travel times.		x	x			x (BCR > 1)	Travel time
Reduce user costs.		x					User fees
Reduce work-zone impacts during construction and maintenance.		x	x				Travel time
Reduce loss of emergency services or avoid emergency management costs.	x		x			x	Delays, administrative costs
Avoid NFIP administration costs.	x						Administrative costs
Increase economic or labor market opportunities because of new connections between communities.			x	x			Jobs, income, income tax
Increase land or property value in nearby communities.			x	x	x		Property value
Prevent displacement of residents.	x		x	x	x		Temporary housing or relocation costs
Improve housing affordability.				x	x		Housing costs, units
Improve recreational value.						x (BCR > 1)	Recreational visits
Mitigate other social or economic impacts.	x (BCR > 0.75)					x	Income, wages

66

TABLE 5.6

Environmental and Physical Benefits Included in Various Federal Agency BCA Guidance Documents

Benefit	Agency and Program						Metric
	FEMA	FAA AIP	DOT RAISE	HUD CDBG-DR or CDBG-NDRC	HUD CDBG-MIT	HMGP	
Environmental							
Improve natural environment (i.e., environmental quality).	x			x	x	x	Area of habitat or coastal restoration; acres of wetland; air or water quality; tree cover
Mitigate existing ecological or environmental impacts.		x	x	x	x		Area of habitat or coastal restoration; acres of wetland; air or water quality; tree cover; reduction in heat index
Reduce emissions.		x	x	x			Emissions
Reduce noise pollution.		x	x				Noise (decibels)
Physical							
Mitigate a natural hazard (i.e., resilience).	x	x				x	Injuries and deaths, property damage, loss of critical facilities, energy and water outages, road closures, site contamination, damage to historical or cultural resources
Improve operational reliability (e.g., loss of public services or utilities, reduced delays, schedule predictability).	x	x	x	x	x		Energy and water outages, lost income or wages, time delays, road or bridge closures
Improve infrastructure capacity.		x	x			x (BCR > 1)	Number of vehicles, number or size of aircraft or vessels, water supply or hydropower
Divert a transportation mode.			x				Highway congestion, value of pavement damage caused by trucks, emissions
Save operating cost (e.g., reduced facility maintenance costs).		x	x	x		x	Long-term operation and maintenance costs, energy costs

ria and project prioritization, along with other factors. This provides an opportunity to appropriately weight nonmonetized benefits in the evaluation process to address equity considerations, rather than automatically disqualifying any project that does not have a BCR greater than 1.

Finally, FEMA and other agencies have different levels of interaction with and deference to OMB examiners in award selection. Most agencies have limited interaction with OMB examiners for individual project awards, whereas FEMA has a systematic process of submitting every project-level subapplication over $1 million to OMB for review.[19] Because of the strict interpretation of the 7-percent real discount rate and because certain benefits cannot be monetized, FEMA's interactions generally limit its ability to award grants to applicants that do not (or cannot) conduct formal BCA or have a BCR less than 1.

Informed by these analyses, we highlight the following findings with respect to BCA across various federal grant programs:

- Most non-DoD agencies have established a minimum project cost threshold below which applicants are not required to perform formal BCA *or* the minimum award amount is sufficiently high that lower-cost projects would not be affected.
- The types of benefits allowed for consideration in BCAs vary across federal programs because of the nature of the projects.
  - Interviewees from most agencies expressed interest in considering as wide a variety of benefits as possible. In some cases, interviewees said that particular categories of benefits were not relevant to their programs' objectives or expressed the need for caution to avoid erroneously categorizing transfers as benefits.
  - Some agencies limit the time horizon over which benefits are calculated because uncertainty about the future, even if projects assets have a longer useful lifetime, while other agencies encourage applicants to use a longer time horizon when calculating benefits to better reflect community preferences.
- Across the federal government, most discretionary grant programs and infrastructure planning agencies have policies and procedures in place to allow nonmonetized benefits to be considered in the evaluation of alternatives and eligibility criteria. In most cases, there are exceptions that allow awards for a project that has a BCR of less than 1 if there are reasonable anticipated benefits than cannot be easily quantified.
- Agencies generally follow OMB's directive to use a 7-percent discount rate to apply to the base-case analysis. However, some agencies have interpreted OMB's guidance to evaluate alternatives to allow the use of different discount rates.
  - Most agencies give applicants flexibility to use lower discount rates with justification, particularly with regard to environmental or social benefits that might accrue over a long time horizon.
  - Some agencies stated that the discount rate should reflect a community's preference for trade-offs between current and future benefits. Others said that Circular A-94 clearly prescribed the use of a 7-percent discount rate with little room for alternative interpretations.
  - Water resource planning agencies (e.g., USACE) use specified discount rates that are set annually, by law.

Chapter 6 presents options for FEMA based on these findings and other findings presented in this report.

---

[19] FEMA staff, interview with the authors, June 2022.

Possible Changes to the Use of BCA in the Hazard Mitigation Assistance Grant Process

FEMA's HMA grants help communities mitigate the potential negative consequences of disasters. However, as discussed in Chapter 1, there is some concern that not all communities have equal access to FEMA resources. In particular, there is evidence that disadvantaged communities, broadly defined, might be less likely to receive such federal grants. BCA has been identified as a potential reason for such inequality.

In this report, we highlight two mechanisms through which BCA might cause HMA grants to be inequitably distributed. First, the complexity of the application process might dissuade communities with fewer resources from applying for HMA grants at all. Second, BCA's focus on monetary impacts might cause the processes of selecting HMA grant recipients to favor areas with higher property values. We cannot definitively confirm or reject the existence or effects of either mechanism.

FEMA faces two potentially conflicting pressures as it considers approaches to address this concern. On one hand, communities have provided FEMA with feedback that reinforces the concern that the complexity of the grant application process dissuades low-resource communities from applying. On the other hand, the budget oversight officials have requested more and more-detailed sensitivity analyses of the values the BCA process uses as an input. FEMA offers tools and support services to help applicants navigate the grant application process, but the extent of support that FEMA can offer is constrained by staffing and budget limitations.

This chapter combines the evidence and context presented throughout this report to identify nine changes that FEMA could implement to address inequities introduced by the use of BCA in the HMA grant process. We organize these options into three broad categories: Simplify the application process, revise how costs and benefits are considered, and other changes. These options are not mutually exclusive; FEMA could elect to implement a combination of these options. In some cases, implementing one option would alter the ways in which another option might be implemented. In this report, we focus on the identification of options; we did not investigate potential implementation approaches. HSOAC and FEMA are continuing to work together following the release of this report to further explore potential implementation approaches.

We also acknowledge that these options would not be implemented in a static environment. FEMA is already exploring and, in some cases, implementing changes to its HMA grants that are intended to support equitable access to HMA funds. These include pilot programs for both BRIC and FMA grants in relation to meeting the Justice40 Initiative, a proposed removal of the restriction on the extent to which social and economic impacts can be used to meet the HMA program's BCR threshold, and offering additional technical support to applicants.

Simplify the Application Process

Option 1: Replace BCA with a Simpler Measure of Cost-Effectiveness

As discussed in Chapter 4, the relevant authorities clearly support the application of a less rigorous cost-effectiveness analysis rather than the more complex, and more burdensome, BCA. The Stafford Act and its corresponding regulations at C.F.R., Title 44, Part 206, specifically require a cost-effectiveness analysis for HMA grant evaluations. Additionally, Justice40 Initiative EOs 14008 and 13985 require FEMA to remove or reduce complexities and burdens from the HMA grant process in order to increase the equitable access and delivery of mitigation grant benefits to disadvantaged communities. Simpler application requirements could increase the number of applications from communities that previously found the process too complex or burdensome.

FEMA has chosen to use BCA to establish cost-effectiveness, but the agency has the authority to issue new policy guidance to change the methodology used to do so. For example, FEMA could use that authority to replace the BCA requirement with a threshold analysis, under which an applicant needs to prove only that benefits exceed costs (or the BCR passes some other threshold). Additional quantification of benefits would not be required. As discussed in Chapter 2, such a change would largely formalize what applicants appear to already be doing—seeking to cross the BCR threshold without pursuing quantification of additional, unrewarded benefits.

Option 2: Establish a Minimum Cost Threshold or Other Criteria for a Full BCA

As discussed in Chapter 5, most non-DoD agencies have established minimum project cost thresholds below which an applicant is not required to perform a formal BCA or the minimum award amount is sufficiently high that lower-cost projects would not be affected. A minimum cost threshold could address some equity considerations in removing a significant barrier to low-income or vulnerable communities that do not have the resources to prepare a complex economic analysis (or determine that quantifying certain benefits is too difficult). Alternatively, some agencies use other criteria, such as project type, to determine which projects require formal BCA.

This is also a matter of practicality and cost-effectiveness in the grant allocation process. Conducting a BCA is not free; hiring a consultant to conduct a BCA can cost a community hundreds of thousands of dollars. If the costs of conducting a BCA are considered as part of the cost of small projects, requiring a BCA can easily cause a small project to become no longer cost-effective, and small, disadvantaged communities could decline to submit applications for this reason. Per option 1, a simpler measure of cost-effectiveness, such as narrative descriptions of benefits, could be used for smaller projects, with cost-effectiveness being determined at a programmatic level.

This change could increase the number of projects submitted to FEMA. It might also reduce the number of projects that are rejected for not meeting the cost-effectiveness requirement (as currently interpreted by FEMA as having a BCR of 1 using a 7-percent discount rate) but otherwise achieve one or more of FEMA's statutory objectives. Therefore, it could affect the fraction of awards granted to lower-income or disadvantaged communities. Finally, it would reduce the administrative burden of reviewing and adjudicating applications for smaller projects.

Revise How Costs and Benefits Are Considered

Option 3: Allow Applicants to Include Alternative Discount Rates

As discussed in Chapter 5, some agencies allow applicants to consider alternative discount rates in addition to the 7 percent advised by OMB Circular A-94. As discussed in Chapter 1, the FEMA and the NAC have expressed concerns that the choice of interest rate is disproportionately preventing lower-resourced or less urban communities from surpassing the 1 BCR threshold. The extent to which changes to the BCR would affect the pool of eligible HMA subapplicants is not clear; they might be likelier to change the types of projects submitted than to change the types of communities that benefit. On one hand, the role of property values could make it more difficult for poorer or rural communities to obtain the dense, high-value benefits necessary to surpass a 1 BCR, particularly at an overestimated discount rate. On the other hand, our analysis of the distribution of BCRs suggests that most applicants already reach the 1 BCR threshold while still leaving some benefits unquantified (although this might represent a selection bias), and changes to the interest rate do not directly affect the simplicity of the BCA process (other than by allowing subapplicants to leave more benefits unquantified while still reaching a BCR of 1). Regardless, FEMA has the legal authority to provide alternative guidance on interest rates if desired; neither the legal authorities nor OMB Circular A-94 prescribe that FEMA must use a 7-percent discount rate when evaluating the future value presented by grant applicants.[1] FEMA could provide applicants with guidance on when an alternative discount rate might be appropriate, provided either in addition to the 7-percent rate as a sensitivity test or as a replacement to the 7-percent rate altogether.

Using a discount rate that exceeds a community's true future discount rate would underestimate the long-run benefits relative to up-front costs, resulting in an erroneously low BCR. Conversely, a discount rate that is too low would result in an erroneously high BCR. The ideal discount rate would accurately reflect the present value of future costs and benefits to that community, plus a premium that reflects the risk of project benefits not accruing.

Unfortunately, precisely quantifying this theoretically ideal discount rate, which likely varies across time, communities, and projects, is not possible. Thus the most practical approach might simply be to consider multiple interest rates to illustrate the extent to which the choice of interest rate influences the cost-effectiveness calculation. FEMA could suggest a particular interest rate to use for such a comparison, or each applicant could offer and justify its own. In either case, interest rate should be selected based on its ability to reflect the present value of future costs and the risk around realizing predicted benefits, rather than based on efforts to influence the particular types of projects that receive funding.

There are several reference points beyond the fixed discount rate of 7 percent that has long been advised by OMB Circular A-94. U.S. Treasury rates reflect the present value of future costs in a relatively minimal-risk setting. Municipal bonds issued by a community reflect the true present value of future financial costs to the community were the community to fund the project itself. A community might use these or other rates as reference points for identifying two or more interest rates that would illustrate the extent to which its project's cost-effectiveness is reliant on the weight of near-term costs and benefits versus far-off costs and benefits. Forcing applicants to use only a 7-percent discount rate might not result in an accurate or full reflection of

---

[1] OMB Circular A-94 states that the use of 7 percent is intended to promote efficient investment and account for the displacement of private investments and consumption, noting that "[t]his rate approximates the marginal pretax rate of return on an average investment in the private sector in recent years." As a result, a discount rate of 7 percent requires HMA grant applicants to demonstrate the same rate of return as private investments did when OMB Circular A-94 was originally released in 1992. It is not obvious that an investment in a public good many decades later should necessarily be expected or intended to exhibit the same rate of return.

the extent to which a project's cost-effectiveness is reliant on this trade-off between near-term and far-off costs and benefits.

Option 4: Consider Broader Types of Benefits

As discussed in Chapter 5, the benefits allowed by different discretionary grant programs and infrastructure planning agencies vary; not all types of benefits are allowable under each agency's BCA criteria, but all are paid for by federal grant dollars. At a programmatic level, this difference in evaluation criteria is a common reflection of programs' differing goals. But in terms of nationwide policy, this creates inconsistency in terms of federal dollars being restricted to supporting only certain types of benefits depending on the source of the federal funds. Although this differential treatment of federal dollars might be efficient if agencies have differing abilities to access particular types of benefits or if policy preferences dictate that funds focus on specific uses, these limitations on benefit categories could also limit an applicant's ability to surpass BCR thresholds even if the project was desirable from a federalwide perspective. Specifically, such benefits as quality-of-life improvements, economic or labor market opportunities, value of time savings, and reduced emissions or energy costs are permitted to be counted in only certain programs and contexts, despite being broadly desirable.

Some agencies accept broader categories of benefits than others. HUD's process allows grantees to use any BCA that has been approved by USACE, DOT, or FEMA. In addition, most programs have policies and procedures in place to allow nonmonetized benefits to be considered in the evaluation of alternatives and eligibility criteria. Specifically, agencies have implemented processes to award discretionary grants to projects that did not meet the minimum BCR requirement by either providing an alternative demonstration (i.e., qualitative discussion) of benefits or weighing environmental concerns, cultural or historical significance, interconnectivity, or other factors among the evaluation criteria. However, others have cautioned that particular categories of benefits might not be relevant to program objectives and that creative efforts to identify benefits can easily lead to errors, such as double-counting and erroneously categorizing transfers as benefits.

Option 5: Apply Distributional Weights to Benefit and Cost Calculations

As discussed in Chapter 3, some critics of the HMA grant process have argued that current methods to evaluate distribution of benefits overweight certain benefit components, such as property value, relative to other potential benefits, such as human health or well-being (Junod et al., 2021). At the heart of this criticism is a belief that benefits and costs of HMA programs are not distributed optimally or equitably among the population of interest. Scholars have noted that prevailing BCA methods, such as those commonly used by federal agencies, are insensitive to distributional concerns in that they do not explicitly consider whether policy beneficiaries have lower (or higher) incomes or lower (or higher) levels of other welfare-relevant attributes than others in the population (Adler, 2016). In response to this issue, some scholars have argued that valuing costs or benefits differently for different groups is more accurate and theoretically grounded (Aldy and Viscusi, 2007; Sunstein, 2004). However, such an approach remains controversial: Others argue that such treatment inappropriately codifies implicit or explicit biases into federal policy (Goodwin, 2020). A previous effort by the U.S. Environmental Protection Agency to calculate different values of statistical life for different age groups met with significant political backlash (Seelye and Tierney, 2003). Still others argue that both points are true and that the solution is to impose additional distributional weights to resolve the inherent inequities imposed by theoretically sound but ethically undesirable differentiations (Adler, 2016).

One option for addressing concerns about inequity in the distribution of HMA grants is for FEMA to consider a distributional weight system that directly incorporates policy preferences around the distribution of federal funds into weights that influence the value assigned to the benefits and costs presented in an application. However, this involves replacing an implicit set of preferences around distributional concerns with an explicit one. To avoid unintended creation of new inequities, policymakers would need to be careful to ensure that any weighting scheme aligned appropriately with the inequities that the policy intended to address. A distributional weight scheme would also need to avoid falling afoul of rules regarding what factors can and cannot be used to discriminate between applicants in the distribution of federal funds. And care would need to be taken to address or manage backlash from disaffected stakeholders. Furthermore, any implementation of distributional weights should be done in a manner that avoids increasing the complexity of the application process because that could result in unintended increases in inequity if disadvantaged applicants are disproportionately deterred by complex application processes.

Other Changes

Option 6: Incorporate BCA and BCR More Clearly into the Award Decision

As discussed in Chapter 2, HMA applications' BCRs are currently considered only for the purpose of determining eligibility. This makes the BCA a threshold analysis in practice, and gives applicants little incentive to carefully document all possible benefits. Because not all eligible applicants receive funding, this behavior could result in inefficient allocations of federal funds. As discussed in Chapter 4, most (not all) federal entities use BCRs as part of an eligibility threshold. Some federal entities, such as DOT and USACE, more explicitly incorporate net benefits or BCRs into the award decision process, although no agency bases its grant allocation decisions solely on applications' net benefits or BCRs.

FEMA could similarly incorporate the BCR or other aspects of BCA more fully into the evaluation process. This change would not address FEMA's concerns about complexity but would incentivize applicants to more fully document project benefits. This option might or might not be incompatible with option 1, depending on whether an alternative measure of cost-effectiveness is still able to provide a relative ranking of project benefits or BCRs.

Option 7: Change FEMA Large Project Notification Reporting Practices

The FY 2022 Consolidated Appropriations Act (Pub. L. 117-103) requires FEMA to notify Congress of awards greater than $1 million no later than three business days prior to the grant or project funds being obligated.[2] Although it is not required to do so, FEMA currently submits projects above the LPN threshold to OMB for review prior to submitting to Congress or even DHS leadership. This review process typically takes approximately one week and does not appear to be imposing significant problems, although, in rare instances, OMB has requested additional information that delayed funding of projects by months.[3]

As explained in Chapter 3, the Budget Control Act of 2011 does not require FEMA to provide such notifications to OMB. As we illustrate in Chapter 4, FEMA's relationship with OMB is unusual in comparison to all other federal agencies with whose representatives we spoke in relation to project-level review. FEMA could consider suspending its practice of deferring to OMB's substantive review of these grant awards because this practice is not required or supported by legal, regulatory, or executive branch policy (i.e., OMB Circular A-94)

---

[2] FEMA staff, conversations with the authors, June 29, 2022. The purpose of these notifications appears to be promotion rather than oversight. The reporting process focuses on providing notification to the representatives of awarded communities. We are not aware of any situation in which congressional notification has led to concerns or delays.

[3] FEMA staff, conversations with the authors, June 29, 2022.

authorities. The authorities do not prohibit FEMA from considering OMB review and feedback, but OMB lacks authority to require its substantive review or its concurrence, approval, or denial of grant applications.

Option 8: Precisely Specify Benefiting Areas

As discussed in Chapter 3, determining which communities benefit from a given HMA-funded project is of crucial importance for equity and Justice40 outcomes. Historically, HMA programs have not collected precise or standardized information about the benefiting area of a project. Although such tools as the CEJST and SVI provide metrics of disadvantaged status at the census tract level, HMA programs do not systematically collect information about project beneficiaries at a geographic level any more granular than the county. This is problematic because the benefits of hazard mitigation projects rarely flow in perfect alignment with county boundaries. By precisely specifying the benefiting areas of projects in subapplications, with a focus on census tract–level information for analytical consistency with available federal tools, such as SVI and the CEJST, FEMA can better ensure that program benefits flow as intended with regard to objectives, such as the Justice40 goal of delivering 40 percent of benefits to disadvantaged communities.

Option 9: Encourage Applicants to Solicit Subapplications from Disadvantaged Communities

As discussed in Chapters 2 and 3, available evidence suggests that a key challenge to meeting equity goals might be the lack of applications from disadvantaged communities. Once FEMA has developed a durable metric (e.g., SVI, the CEJST) with which to measure and assign disadvantaged status to communities applying for HMA program funds, FEMA might more proactively and strategically engage with disadvantaged communities to notify them of Justice40 goals and HMA program funding availability to encourage new subapplications from qualifying communities that have not previously participated in HMA programs. Given the level of discretion and influence that applicants (typically states, territories, or federally recognized tribes) have in the HMGP process, FEMA could consider developing additional guidance and deepening coordination with applicant partners to ensure that such objectives as those legally required by the Justice40 Initiative discussed in Chapter 4 are met.

Compliance with the Administrative Procedure Act

We found that the options above do not require legislative or regulatory action. They are steps that FEMA could take pursuant to its current legal, regulatory, and discretionary policy authorities. Even if FEMA decides to no longer require grant applications to have a BCA greater than or equal to 1, implementation of that change—and other options described in this report—could trigger certain legal obligations for the agency under the APA.

To implement the options above, FEMA would need to amend, change, or revise its policies and procedures for administering the HMA grant programs. This could include initiating the appropriate processes and procedures to develop and issue new policy documents (e.g., directives, instructions, memoranda, manuals, and SOPs). Under the APA, federal agencies must meet certain standards and take certain actions as part of the policymaking or rulemaking process, including existing policies and rules (see Garvey, 2017, p. 1).

In many instances, the APA sets forth informal rulemaking procedures, which generally include the agency publishing new rules and rule changes in the *Federal Register*, such as the issuance of notices and a public comment period (and comment adjudication) prior to establishing a final rule (U.S. Code, Title 5, Section 553[b]). However, agency matters related to grants or benefits are exempt from this informal process

(U.S. Code, Title 5, Section 553[a][2]). Additionally, "interpretive rules, general statements of policy, and rules of agency organization, procedure, or practice" are exempt from the formal process (U.S. Code, Title 5, Section 553[b][A]):

> Interpretive rules are statements of general applicability and future effect that set forth an agency's interpretation of a statute or regulation. General statements of policy set forth an agency's policy on a statutory, regulatory, or technical issue—for example, the agency's intended posture on enforcement priorities. (Bowers, 2021, p. 1)

Therefore, it is very likely that changes to the application of the BCA, the 7-percent discount rate, and the LPN trigger for OMB review fall into the category of an interpretive rule (i.e., an interpretation of the statutory term *cost-effective*) or a general statement of policy on statutory, regulatory, or technical issues (i.e., the adjudication of HMA grant applications).

Notwithstanding exemption from the formal rulemaking process, when an agency makes a "significant policy change or other reversal, the agency is required to comply with applicable APA procedural requirements."[4] Specifically, the agency must ensure that the change in policy is not "arbitrary, capricious, an abuse of discretion, or otherwise not in accordance with law."[5]

To avoid violation (or perceived violation) of the APA's requirement for agencies to abide by their own regulations and policies, an agency must—when it changes its policies—do the following:

- **Publicly acknowledge that it is changing its policy.** "An agency action that departs from a prior policy without acknowledging the change, or that creates an 'unexplained inconsistency' with prior policy is generally viewed as arbitrary and capricious" (Garvey, 2017, p. 16).
- **Publicly explain the reasons for the change in its policy.** "An agency 'need not demonstrate . . . that the reasons for the new policy are better than the reasons for the old one . . .'" (Garvey, 2017, p. 16, citing *FCC*, 2009, at 515). Additionally, "it is enough for the agency to show that there are 'good reasons' for the change and that the 'new policy is permissible under the statute'" (Garvey, 2017, p. 16).
- **Provide a "more detailed justification" for the change in policy** if (1) new factual findings contradict those underlying the old policy or (2) the previous policy "engendered serious reliance interests that must be taken into account" (Garvey, 2017, p. 16, citing *FCC*, 2009, at 515–516).[6] "In each instance, the [Supreme] Court noted that it would be arbitrary and capricious to 'ignore' or 'disregard' such matters" (Garvey, 2017, p. 16, citing *FCC*, 2009, at 516).[7]

Given that FEMA's current policy has been to apply a BCA and a 7-percent discount rate has been in place for decades,[8] if FEMA makes these changes, supportive steps by FEMA would include formally, and publicly, issuing a change to these policies and accompanying that issuance with a detailed public explanation for the

---

[4] See Garvey, 2017, p. 15, citing *Perez*, 2015, at 101 (holding that the APA "mandate[s] that agencies use the same procedures when they amend or repeal a rule as they used to issue the rule in the first instance").

[5] See U.S. Code, Title 5, Section 706(2)(A). The "arbitrary and capricious" standard is the standard of review that a court would apply to determine whether the agency's change in policy was lawful.

[6] See also *Encino Motorcars, LLC v. Navarro*, 136 S. Ct. (2016) at 2125 .

[7] Also citing *Encino Motorcars* (2016) at 2126–2127 (holding that a summary explanation of an agency's reasons for changing its position "may suffice in other circumstance" but that, when there have been decades of industry reliance on a policy, an agency must present "a more reasoned explanation" for "why it deemed it necessary to overrule its previous position").

[8] FEMA SMEs, interviews with the authors, 2021 and 2022.

reasons for the change. All three required actions above could be accomplished with the publication of a new FEMA directive, instruction, policy memorandum, or other formal statement of FEMA policy.

Further Considerations and Limitations

The options presented in this section offer a variety of ways in which FEMA might improve equity of access to HMA funds. To support the design and implementation of these options, FEMA should also consider identifying metrics for documenting and measuring the success of these or other efforts to address inequality. Such metrics could provide insights that support the design of additional interventions and provide program-level data to determine whether concerns about inequity have been addressed. Identifying such metrics was beyond the scope of this report.

This report does not fully explore the complexities and challenges that could be involved in implementing these options. It is our intention that FEMA be able to consider these options and identify those which appear best suited to the needs of the HMA programs; hence the label of "options" rather than "recommendations." HSOAC and FEMA are continuing to work together to understand how these options might be implemented. Those additional insights will be provided at a later date in an addendum to this report.

Our Semistructured Interview Protocol

Our BCA Study: Semistructured Interview Questions, April 2022

1. Can you briefly describe your agency's or program's goals and general project evaluation framework?
2. What types of projects require a formal BCA?
   a. Does your agency or program have a statutory requirement or formal policy to demonstrate project cost-effectiveness or conduct a BCA?
   b. Are any types of projects exempt from this requirement?
   c. Is there a project cost threshold below which projects are not required to conduct a BCA?
3. What guidance documents do agency or program staff or applicants rely on to prepare project BCAs?
4. How has your agency or program standardized or streamlined the application or project evaluation process?
   a. What types of benefits and costs are allowable in the BCA?
   b. What, if any, planning tools (e.g., standardized methods, precalculated benefits or costs) are available?
   c. Has your agency or program made any changes to make it easier to prepare a BCA?
   d. What form of assistance does your agency or program provide to help applicants complete a BCA?
   e. Has your agency or program made any specific changes with equity considerations in mind to diversify the composition of applicants or awards?
5. How does your BCA review process account for benefits or costs that cannot be easily monetized?
   a. What guidance or options does your agency or program provide for presenting qualitative (non-monetized) benefits?
   b. If the monetized benefits of a project do not exceed its costs, is there a mechanism for qualitative (nonmonetized) benefits to factor into project eligibility or award decisions?
6. What statutory or regulatory authorities does your agency or program rely on with respect to cost-effectiveness requirements (e.g., discount rates)?
   a. How does your agency or program interpret the discount rate requirements of OMB Circular A-94?
   b. What discount rates are analysts or applicants permitted to use in the BCA?
   c. What options, if any, are available to use alternative discount rates in the BCA?
7. If a project meets all of the eligibility criteria (e.g., has a BCR of 1 or greater), what additional criteria are used evaluate projects and select awards?
   a. Is the BCR (or net benefit) a criterion in the evaluation process?

8. What is OMB's role in the BCA review process?

   a. What type of review, if any, does the OMB examiner for your agency or program conduct for individual projects?

   b. What process does your agency or program follow if the OMB examiner raises a question or point of disagreement?

Abbreviations

AIP	Airport Improvement Program
APA	Administrative Procedure Act
APP	area of persistent poverty
BCA	benefit–cost analysis
BCR	benefit–cost ratio
BRIC	Building Resilient Infrastructure and Communities
CDBG	Community Development Block Grant
CDBG-DR	Community Development Block Grant Disaster Recovery
CDBG-MIT	Community Development Block Grant Mitigation
CDBG-NDR	Community Development Block Grant National Disaster Resilience
CDC	Centers for Disease Control and Prevention
CEJST	Climate and Economic Justice Screening Tool
CEQ	Council on Environmental Quality
C.F.R.	Code of Federal Regulations
DHS	U.S. Department of Homeland Security
DoD	U.S. Department of Defense
DOT	U.S. Department of Transportation
DRF	Disaster Relief Fund
EDRC	economically disadvantaged rural community
EHP	environmental and historic preservation
EO	executive order
FAA	Federal Aviation Administration
FEMA	Federal Emergency Management Agency
FIMA	Federal Insurance and Mitigation Administration
FMA	Flood Mitigation Assistance (program)
FY	fiscal year
HDC	historically disadvantaged community
HMA	hazard mitigation assistance
HMGP	Hazard Mitigation Grant Program
HSOAC	Homeland Security Operational Analysis Center
HUD	U.S. Department of Housing and Urban Development
LMI	low to moderate income
LPN	large project notification

NAC	National Advisory Council
NED	national economic development
NFIP	National Flood Insurance Program
NOFA	notice of funding availability
NOFO	notice of funding opportunity
NSI	National Structure Inventory
OMB	Office of Management and Budget
PD	presidential declaration
PDM	predisaster mitigation
PDMGP	Pre-Disaster Mitigation Grant Program
P&G	*Economic and Environmental Principles and Guidelines for Water and Related Land Resources Implementation Studies*
PR&G	*Principles and Requirements for Federal Investments in Water Resources* and *Final Interagency Guidelines*
P&S	*Principles and Standards for Planning Water and Related Land Resources*
PUL	project useful life
RAISE	Rebuilding American Infrastructure with Sustainability and Equity
SME	subject-matter expert
SOP	standard operating procedure
SVI	Social Vulnerability Index
SWF	social welfare function
TIGER	Transportation Investment Generating Economic Recovery
UK	United Kingdom
USACE	U.S. Army Corps of Engineers

References

Adler, Matthew D., *Well-Being and Fair Distribution: Beyond Cost–Benefit Analysis*, Oxford University Press, 2011.

Adler, Matthew D., "Benefit–Cost Analysis and Distributional Weights: An Overview," *Review of Environmental Economics*, Vol. 10, No. 2, 2016.

Agency for Toxic Substances and Disease Registry, Centers for Disease Control and Prevention, "CDC's Social Vulnerability Index (SVI): SVI Interactive Map," webpage, page last reviewed October 9, 2018. As of July 25, 2022:
https://svi.cdc.gov/map.html

Agency for Toxic Substances and Disease Registry, "CDC/ATSDR SVI Data and Documentation Download," webpage, last reviewed August 27, 2021. As of September 9, 2022:
https://www.atsdr.cdc.gov/placeandhealth/svi/data_documentation_download.html

Aldy, Joseph E., and W. Kip Viscusi, "Age Differences in the Value of Statistical Life: Revealed Preference Evidence," *Review of Environmental Economics and Policy*, Vol. 1, No. 1, 2007.

Arrow, Kenneth J., *Social Choice and Individual Values*, Wiley and Sons, 1951.

Auer v. Robbins, 519 U.S. 452, 1997.

Biden, Joseph R., Jr., "Executive Order 13985 of January 20, 2021: Advancing Racial Equity and Support for Underserved Communities Through the Federal Government," *Federal Register*, Vol. 86, No. 14, January 25, 2021a.

Biden, Joseph R., Jr., "Executive Order 14008 of January 27, 2021: Tackling the Climate Crisis at Home and Abroad," *Federal Register*, Vol. 86, No. 19, February 1, 2021b.

Bowers, Kate R., *Agency Use of Guidance Documents*, Congressional Research Service, LSB10591, April 19, 2021.

Budget Control Act—*See* Public Law 112-25, 2011.

Bush, Eric Lawrence, acting chief, Planning and Policy Division, Directorate of Civil Works, U.S. Army Corps of Engineers, Department of the Army, "Federal Interest Rates for Corps of Engineers Projects for Fiscal Year 2022," Economic Guidance Memorandum 22-01 for the planning community of practice, October 20, 2021.

Carter, Nicole T., and Adam C. Nesbitt, *Discount Rates in the Economic Evaluation of U.S. Army Corps of Engineers Projects*, Congressional Research Service, R44594, updated August 15, 2016.

Carwile, William L., III, associate administrator for response and recovery; David Miller, associate administrator for federal insurance and mitigation; and Edward H. Johnson, acting chief financial officer, Federal Emergency Management Agency, U.S. Department of Homeland Security, "Strategic Funds Management Initiative," memorandum for regional administrators, federal coordinating officers, federal disaster recovery coordinators, regional recovery division directors, regional mitigation division directors, and regional comptrollers, June 11, 2012.

CDBG Program—*See* Community Development Block Grant Program.

CEQ—*See* Council on Environmental Equality.

Chevron, U.S.A., Inc. v. NRDC, Inc., 467 U.S. 837, 1984.

Clinton, William Jefferson, "Executive Order 12893 of January 26, 1994: Principles for Federal Infrastructure Investments," *Federal Register*, Vol. 59, No. 20, January 31, 1994.

Code of Federal Regulations, Title 2, Grants and Agreements; Subtitle A, Office of Management and Budget Guidance for Grants and Agreements; Chapter II, Office of Management and Budget Guidance; Part 200, Uniform Administrative Requirements, Cost Principles, and Audit Requirements for Federal Awards.

Code of Federal Regulations, Title 44, Emergency Management and Assistance.

Committee on Improving Principles and Guidelines for Federal Water Resources Project Planning, Water Science and Technology Board, Division on Earth and Life Sciences, National Research Council of the National Academies, *A Review of the Proposed Revisions to the Federal Principles and Guidelines Water Resources Planning Document*, National Academy Press, 2012.

Committee to Assess the USACE Water Resources Project Planning Procedures—*See* Committee to Assess the U.S. Army Corps of Engineers Water Resources Project Planning Procedures.

Committee to Assess the U.S. Army Corps of Engineers Water Resources Project Planning Procedures, Water Science and Technology Board, Commission on Geosciences, Environment, and Resources, National Research Council of the National Academies, *New Directions in Water Resources Planning of the U.S. Army Corps of Engineers*, National Academy Press, 1999.

Community Development Block Grant Program, Office of Community Planning and Development, U.S. Department of Housing and Urban Development, *Guide to National Objectives and Eligible Activities for Entitlement Communities*, January 2014.

Council on Environmental Quality, "Climate and Economic Justice Screening Tool," webpage, undated. As of July 25, 2022:
https://screeningtool.geoplatform.gov/en/about

Criswell, Deanna, administrator, Federal Emergency Management Agency, U.S. Department of Homeland Security, "Response to National Advisory Council Reports 2020–2021 Recommendations," memorandum for W. Nim Kidd, chair, National Advisory Council, June 3, 2022.

Deputy Associate Administrator for Insurance and Mitigation, Federal Emergency Management Agency, U.S. Department of Homeland Security, *Ecosystem Service Benefits in Benefit–Cost Analysis for FEMA's Mitigation Programs Policy*, Federal Emergency Management Agency Policy 108-024-02, September 28, 2020.

DOT—*See* U.S. Department of Transportation.

Durden, Susan E., and Jim Fredericks, *Economics Primer*, U.S. Army Corps of Engineers, Institute for Water Resources, 09-R-3, June 2009.

Elliott, James R., Phylicia Lee Brown, and Kevin Loughran, "Racial Inequities in Federal Buyouts of Flood-Prone Homes: A Nationwide Assessment of Environmental Adaptation," *Socius*, Vol. 6, 2020.

Encino Motorcars, LLC v. Navarro, 136 S. Ct. 2117, June 20, 2016.

Engineer Research and Development Center, U.S. Army, "Interagency Guidelines," December 2014.

Environmental Defense Fund, *FEMA BRIC Application Best Practices and Recommendations*, March 29, 2022.

EO 12893—*See* Clinton, 1994.

EO 13985—*See* Biden, 2021a.

EO 14008—*See* Biden, 2021b.

FAA—*See* Federal Aviation Administration.

FAA Order 5090.5—*See* Planning and Environmental Division, 2019.

FAA Order 5100.38D—*See* Federal Aviation Administration, 2019.

Farber, Daniel A., and Anne Joseph O'Connell, "Agencies as Adversaries," *California Law Review*, Vol. 105, 2017.

Farrow, Scott, "Environmental Equity and Sustainability: Rejecting the Kaldor–Hicks Criteria," *Ecological Economics*, Vol. 27, No. 2, November 1998.

FCC v. Fox TV Stations, Inc., 556 U.S. 602, April 28, 2009.

Federal Aviation Administration, U.S. Department of Transportation, "Policy and Guidance Regarding Benefit Cost Analysis for Airport Capacity Projects Requesting Discretionary Airport Improvement Program Grant Awards and Letters of Intent," *Federal Register*, Vol. 62, No. 121, June 24, 1997.

Federal Aviation Administration, U.S. Department of Transportation, "Federal Aviation Administration Policy and Final Guidance Regarding Benefit Cost Analysis (BCA) on Airport Capacity Projects for FAA Decisions on Airport Improvement Program (AIP) Discretionary Grants and Letters of Intent (LOI)," *Federal Register*, Vol. 64, No. 240, December 15, 1999.

Federal Aviation Administration, U.S. Department of Transportation, "Terminal Area Operations Aviation Rulemaking Committee," Order 1110.132, February 19, 2002.

Federal Aviation Administration, U.S. Department of Transportation, "Airport Improvement Program History," APP-520, issued November 14, 2017.

Federal Aviation Administration, U.S. Department of Transportation, *Airport Improvement Program Handbook*, Order 5100.38D, change 1, effective February 26, 2019.

Federal Aviation Administration, U.S. Department of Transportation, "Overview: What Is AIP?" webpage, last modified November 2, 2021. As of June 22, 2022:
https://www.faa.gov/airports/aip/overview

Federal Aviation Administration, U.S. Department of Transportation, "Airport Grants Announced on September 22, 2022," c. September 2022.

Federal Emergency Management Agency, U.S. Department of Homeland Security, "Flood Mitigation Assistance," *Federal Register*, Vol. 72, No. 210, October 31, 2007.

Federal Emergency Management Agency, U.S. Department of Homeland Security, *BCA Reference Guide*, June 2009.

Federal Emergency Management Agency, U.S. Department of Homeland Security, *Supplement to the Benefit–Cost Analysis Reference Guide*, June 2011.

Federal Emergency Management Agency, U.S. Department of Homeland Security, "Strategic Funds Management: Implementation Procedures for the Public Assistance Program," Recovery Standard Operating Procedure 9570.24, December 21, 2012.

Federal Emergency Management Agency, U.S. Department of Homeland Security, *Hazard Mitigation Assistance Guidance: Hazard Mitigation Grant Program, Pre-Disaster Mitigation Program, and Flood Mitigation Assistance Program*, February 27, 2015.

Federal Emergency Management Agency, U.S. Department of Homeland Security, "Homeowner's Guide to the Hazard Mitigation Grant Program," November 4, 2016.

Federal Emergency Management Agency, U.S. Department of Homeland Security, *Unit 1: Basic Concepts in Benefit–Cost Analysis (BCA)*, instructor guide, training materials for the 2019 version of the Introduction to Benefit–Cost Analysis classroom course (E/L0276), May 15, 2019a.

Federal Emergency Management Agency, U.S. Department of Homeland Security, *Unit 3: The Benefit–Cost Model*, instructor guide, training materials for the 2019 version of the Introduction to Benefit-Cost Analysis classroom course (E/L0276), June 5, 2019b.

Federal Emergency Management Agency, U.S. Department of Homeland Security, *Summary of Stakeholder Feedback: Building Resilient Infrastructure and Communities (BRIC)*, March 2020a.

Federal Emergency Management Agency, U.S. Department of Homeland Security, "FEMA Launches Building Resilient Infrastructure and Communities," press release, September 25, 2020b.

Federal Emergency Management Agency, U.S. Department of Homeland Security, *Hazard Mitigation Grant Program: Program Overview*, webinar, March 10, 2021a.

Federal Emergency Management Agency, U.S. Department of Homeland Security, *BRIC Qualitative Criteria*, August 2021b.

Federal Emergency Management Agency, U.S. Department of Homeland Security, "Notice of Funding Opportunity: Fiscal Year 2021 Building Resilient Infrastructure and Communities Grants," webpage, last updated August 9, 2021c. As of July 15, 2022:
https://www.fema.gov/fact-sheet/
notice-funding-opportunity-fiscal-year-2021-building-resilient-infrastructure-and

Federal Emergency Management Agency, U.S. Department of Homeland Security, "FEMA's Hazard Mitigation Assistance and Mitigation Planning Regulations," *Federal Register*, Vol. 86, No. 173, September 10, 2021d.

Federal Emergency Management Agency, U.S. Department of Homeland Security, "Before You Apply for Building Resilient Infrastructure and Communities (BRIC) Funds," webpage, last updated November 12, 2021e. As of July 20, 2022:
https://www.fema.gov/grants/mitigation/building-resilient-infrastructure-communities/before-apply

Federal Emergency Management Agency, U.S. Department of Homeland Security, *BRIC Technical Criteria*, December 2021f.

Federal Emergency Management Agency, U.S. Department of Homeland Security, "Building Resilient Infrastructure and Communities FY 2020 Subapplication Status," webpage, last updated December 13, 2021g. As of September 3, 2022:
https://www.fema.gov/grants/mitigation/building-resilient-infrastructure-communities/after-apply/fy-2020-subapplication-status

Federal Emergency Management Agency, U.S. Department of Homeland Security, *The Department of Homeland Security (DHS) Notice of Funding Opportunity (NOFO) Fiscal Year 2022 Flood Mitigation Assistance*, c. 2022a.

Federal Emergency Management Agency, U.S. Department of Homeland Security, "Hazard Mitigation Assistance: Building Resilient Infrastructure and Communities," *Federal Register*, Vol. 87, No. 38, February 25, 2022b.

Federal Emergency Management Agency, U.S. Department of Homeland Security, *FEMA Ecosystem Service Value Updates*, June 2022c.

Federal Emergency Management Agency, U.S. Department of Homeland Security, "Benefit–Cost Analysis Training Materials," webpage, last updated June 3, 2022d. As of July 12, 2022:
https://www.fema.gov/grants/tools/benefit-cost-analysis/training

Federal Emergency Management Agency, U.S. Department of Homeland Security, "How to Perform a Full BCA," webpage, last updated June 3, 2022e. As of January 12, 2023:
https://www.fema.gov/grants/guidance-tools/benefit-cost-analysis/full-bca

Federal Emergency Management Agency, U.S. Department of Homeland Security, "Hazard Mitigation Grant Program," webpage, last updated June 6, 2022f. As of July 11, 2022:
https://www.fema.gov/grants/mitigation/hazard-mitigation

Federal Emergency Management Agency, U.S. Department of Homeland Security, "Flood Mitigation Assistance (FMA) Grant," webpage, last updated June 6, 2022g. As of July 25, 2022:
https://www.fema.gov/grants/mitigation/floods

Federal Emergency Management Agency, U.S. Department of Homeland Security, "Hazard Mitigation Grant Program Post Fire," webpage, last updated June 6, 2022h. As of July 18, 2022:
https://www.fema.gov/grants/mitigation/post-fire

Federal Emergency Management Agency, U.S. Department of Homeland Security, "Hazus," webpage, last updated June 10, 2022i. As of August 15, 2022:
https://www.fema.gov/flood-maps/products-tools/hazus

Federal Emergency Management Agency, U.S. Department of Homeland Security, "BRIC Qualitative Evaluation Criteria," August 2022j.

Federal Emergency Management Agency, U.S. Department of Homeland Security, "Building Resilient Infrastructure and Communities Technical Evaluation Criteria," October 2022k.

Federal Emergency Management Agency, U.S. Department of Homeland Security, "Pre-Disaster Mitigation FY2019 Subapplication Status," webpage, last updated January 10, 2023. As of January 12, 2023:
https://www.fema.gov/grants/mitigation/pre-disaster/pre-disaster-mitigation-fy2019-subapplication-status

Federal Insurance and Mitigation Administration, Federal Emergency Management Agency, U.S. Department of Homeland Security, "Strategic Funds Management Frequently Asked Questions (FAQs)," c. February 24, 2015.

FEMA—*See* Federal Emergency Management Agency.

FIMA—*See* Federal Insurance and Mitigation Administration.

Fleurbaey, Marc, and Rossi Abi-Rafeh, "The Use of Distributional Weights in Benefit–Cost Analysis: Insights from Welfare Economics," *Review of Environmental Economics and Policy*, Vol. 10, No. 2, Summer 2016.

Finucane, Melissa L., Noreen Clancy, Andrew M. Parker, Jessica Welburn Paige, Karishma V. Patel, Devin Tierney, Michael T. Wilson, Peggy Wilcox, Tucker Reese, Jhacova Williams, Jordan R. Reimer, Thomas Edward Goode, Sam Morales, and Alyson Harding, *An Initial Methodology for Evaluating Social Equity Performance in Disaster Mitigation Grants: The Building Resilient Infrastructure and Communities Program*, Homeland Security Operational Analysis Center operated by the RAND Corporation, RR-A2145-1, forthcoming.

Fothergill, Alice, and Lori A. Peek, "Poverty and Disasters in the United States: A Review of Recent Sociological Findings," *Natural Hazards*, Vol. 32, No. 1, May 2004.

Frank, Thomas, "Federal Analysis of Climate Projects 'Similar to Redlining,'" *Climatewire*, July 22, 2021.

Frank, Thomas, "How FEMA Helps White and Rich Americans Escape Floods," *Politico*, May 27, 2022.

GAO—*See* U.S. Government Accountability Office.

Garvey, Todd, *A Brief Overview of Rulemaking and Judicial Review*, Congressional Research Service, R41546, version 13, March 27, 2017.

Gaynor, Pete, administrator, Federal Emergency Management Agency, U.S. Department of Homeland Security, "Response to November 2019 National Advisory Council Recommendations," memorandum for W. Nim Kidd, chair, National Advisory Council, June 23, 2020.

Geistfeld, Mark, "Reconciling Cost–Benefit Analysis with the Principle That Safety Matters More Than Money," *New York University Law Review*, Vol. 76, No. 1, April 2001.

Godschalk, David R., Adam Rose, Elliott Mittler, Keith Porter, and Carol Taylor West, "Estimating the Value of Foresight: Aggregate Analysis of Natural Hazard Mitigation Benefits and Costs," *Journal of Environmental Planning and Management*, Vol. 52, No. 6, 2009.

Goodwin, James, "Cost–Benefit Analysis Is Racist," Center for Progressive Reform, October 9, 2020.

Government of the District of Columbia, "FEMA Hazard Mitigation Assistance Guides: District Government Agency Follow-Up," 2021.

GRA, *Economic Values for FAA Investment and Regulatory Decisions, A Guide*, final report prepared for the Office of Aviation Policy and Plans, Federal Aviation Administration, revised October 3, 2007.

Hausman, Daniel, Michael McPherson, and Debra Satz, *Economic Analysis, Moral Philosophy, and Public Policy*, 3rd ed., Cambridge University Press, 2016.

Hayhoe, Katharine, Donald J. Wuebbles, David R. Easterling, David W. Fahey, Sarah Doherty, James P. Kossin, William V. Sweet, Russell S. Vose, and Michael F. Wehner, "Our Changing Climate," in David Reidmiller, C. W. Avery, David R. Easterling, Kenneth E. Kunkel, K. L. M. Lewis, T. K. Maycock, and B. C. Stewart, eds., *Impacts, Risks, and Adaptation in the United States: Fourth National Climate Assessment*, Vol. II, U.S. Global Change Research Program, 2018.

Hazard Mitigation Assistance Division, Mitigation Directorate, Federal Insurance and Mitigation Administration, Federal Emergency Management Agency, U.S. Department of Homeland Security, "The Department of Homeland Security (DHS) Notice of Funding Opportunity (NOFO) FY 2020 Building Resilient Infrastructure and Communities," c. 2020.

Hazard Mitigation Assistance Division, Mitigation Directorate, Federal Insurance and Mitigation Administration, Federal Emergency Management Agency, U.S. Department of Homeland Security, "The Department of Homeland Security (DHS) Notice of Funding Opportunity (NOFO) Fiscal Year 2021 Flood Mitigation Assistance," c. 2021a.

Hazard Mitigation Assistance Division, Federal Emergency Management Agency, U.S. Department of Homeland Security, "Using Ecosystem Service Benefits in the Benefit–Cost Analysis Policy," fact sheet, January 2021b.

Hazard Mitigation Assistance Division, Mitigation Directorate, Federal Insurance and Mitigation Administration, Federal Emergency Management Agency, U.S. Department of Homeland Security, "The Department of Homeland Security (DHS) Notice of Funding Opportunity (NOFO) Fiscal Year 2022 Building Resilient Infrastructure and Communities," c. 2022.

Headwaters Economics, "Mountain, Midwest, and Gulf States Fail to Secure FEMA Resilience Funding," webpage, July 1, 2021a. As of July 20, 2022:
https://headwaterseconomics.org/natural-hazards/bric-funding/

Headwaters Economics, "Improving Benefit–Cost Analyses for Rural Areas," webpage, November 2021b. As of September 2, 2022:
https://headwaterseconomics.org/equity/improving-benefit-cost-analyses/

Her Majesty's Treasury, *The Green Book: Central Government Guidance on Appraisal and Evaluation*, 2022.

HMA Division—*See* Hazard Mitigation Assistance Division.

Horn, Diane P., *Recent Funding Increases for FEMA Hazard Mitigation Assistance*, Congressional Research Service, IN11733, version 10, July 27, 2022.

Howell, Junia, and James R. Elliott, "Damages Done: The Longitudinal Impacts of Natural Hazards on Wealth Inequality in the United States," *Social Problems*, Vol. 66, No. 3, August 2019.

HUD—*See* U.S. Department of Housing and Urban Development.

Junod, Anne N., Carlos Martín, Rebecca Marx, and Amy Rogin, "Equitable Investment in Resilience: A Review of Benefit–Cost Analysis in Federal Flood Mitigation Infrastructure," Metropolitan Housing and Communities Policy Center, Urban Institute, June 2021.

Kisor v. Wilkie, 139 S. Ct. 2400, June 26, 2019.

Kneese, Allen V., "Economics and Water Resources," in Martin Reuss, ed., *Water Resources Administration in the United States: Policy, Practice, and Emerging Issues*, Michigan State University Press and American Water Resources Association, 1993.

Little, I. M. D., and J. A. Mirrlees, "Project Appraisal and Planning Twenty Years On," *Proceedings of the World Bank Annual Conference on Development Economics 1990*, International Bank for Reconstruction and Development, World Bank, 1991.

Mach, Katharine J., Caroline M. Kraan, Miyuki Hino, A. R. Siders, Erica M. Johnston, and Christopher B. Field, "Managed Retreat Through Voluntary Buyouts of Flood-Prone Properties," *Science Advances*, Vol. 5, No. 10, October 11, 2019.

McCarthy, Francis X., and Natalie Keegan, *FEMA's Pre-Disaster Mitigation Program: Overview and Issues*, Congressional Research Service, RL34537, July 10, 2009.

McGee, Kelly, "A Place Worth Protecting: Rethinking Cost-Benefit Analysis Under FEMA's Flood-Mitigation Programs," *University of Chicago Law Review*, Vol. 88, No. 8, 2021.

Meade, James E., *The Theory of International Economic Policy*, Vol. II: *Trade and Welfare*, Oxford University Press, 1955.

Miller, Benjamin M., Debra Knopman, Liisa Ecola, Brian Phillips, Moon Kim, Nathaniel Edenfield, Daniel Schwam, and Diogo Prosdocimi, *U.S. Airport Infrastructure Funding and Financing: Issues and Policy Options Pursuant to Section 122 of the 2018 Federal Aviation Administration Reauthorization Act*, RAND Corporation, RR-3175-FAA, 2020. As of January 13, 2023:
https://www.rand.org/pubs/research_reports/RR3175.html

Motor Vehicle Manufacturers Association v. State Farm Auto Manual Insurance Co., 463 U.S. 29, 1983.

Multi-Hazard Mitigation Council, National Institute of Building Sciences, *Natural Hazard Mitigation Saves: 2019 Report*, December 2019.

NAC—*See* National Advisory Council.

National Advisory Council, Federal Emergency Management Agency, *Report to the FEMA Administrator*, November 2019.

National Advisory Council, Federal Emergency Management Agency, *Report to the FEMA Administrator*, November 2020.

National Advisory Council, Federal Emergency Management Agency, *Report to the FEMA Administrator*, December 2021.

National Archives and Records Administration, "Implementation of Uniform Administrative Requirements, Cost Principles, and Audit Requirements for Federal Awards," *Federal Register*, Vol. 80, No. 164, August 25, 2015.

National Centers for Environmental Information, National Oceanic and Atmospheric Administration, "Billion-Dollar Weather and Climate Disasters," webpage, undated. As of July 27, 2022:
https://www.ncei.noaa.gov/access/billions/

New York v. Shalala, 959 F. Supp. 614, S.D.N.Y., 1997.

Office of Aviation Policy and Plans, Federal Aviation Administration, U.S. Department of Transportation, *FAA Airport Benefit–Cost Analysis Guidance*, September 16, 2020.

Office of Management and Budget, Executive Office of the President, "Legislative Coordination and Clearance," Circular A-19, September 20, 1979.

Office of Management and Budget, Executive Office of the President, "Guidelines and Discount Rates for Benefit–Cost Analysis of Federal Programs," Circular A-94, October 29, 1992.

Office of Management and Budget, Executive Office of the President, "Regulatory Analysis," Circular A-4, September 17, 2003.

Office of Management and Budget, Executive Office of President, "Cost Principles for State, Local, and Indian Tribal Governments," Circular A-87, revised May 10, 2004.

Office of Management and Budget, Executive Office of the President, "Preparation, Submission, and Execution of the Budget," Circular A-11, July 2016.

Office of Management and Budget, Executive Office of the President; U.S. Department of Health and Human Services; Farm Service Agency, Commodity Credit Corporation, National Institute of Food and Agriculture, Rural Utilities Service, Rural Business–Cooperative Service, Rural Housing Service, Rural Utilities Service, Farm Service Agency, U.S. Department of Agriculture; U.S. Department of State; U.S. Agency for International Development; U.S. Department of Veterans Affairs; U.S. Department of Energy; U.S. Department of Treasury; U.S. Department of Defense; U.S. Department of Transportation; U.S. Department of Commerce; U.S. Department of the Interior; U.S. Environmental Protection Agency; National Aeronautics and Space Administration; Corporation for National and Community Service; Social Security Administration; U.S. Department of Housing And Urban Development; National Science Foundation; National Archives and Records Administration; U.S. Small Business Administration; U.S. Department of Justice; U.S. Department of Labor; Federal Emergency Management Agency, U.S. Department of Homeland Security; Institute of Museum and Library Services; National Endowment for the Arts; National Endowment for the Humanities; U.S. Department of Education; Office of National Drug Control Policy, Executive Office of the President; and Gulf Coast Ecosystem Restoration Council, "Federal Awarding Agency Regulatory Implementation of Office of Management and Budget's Uniform Administrative Requirements, Cost Principles, and Audit Requirements for Federal Awards," *Federal Register*, Vol. 79, No. 244, December 19, 2014.

Office of Operations, Freight Management and Operations, Federal Highway Administration, U.S. Department of Transportation, "RAISE–BUILD–TIGER Discretionary Grants," webpage, updated February 22, 2022. As of July 18, 2022:
https://ops.fhwa.dot.gov/freight/infrastructure/tiger/

Office of the Secretary, U.S. Department of Transportation, *Benefit–Cost Analysis Guidance for Discretionary Grant Programs*, revised, March 2022.

Office of the Secretary, U.S. Department of Transportation, *Notice of Funding Opportunity for the Department of Transportation's National Infrastructure Investments (i.e., the Rebuilding American Infrastructure with Sustainability and Equity (RAISE) Grant Program) under the Infrastructure Investment and Jobs Act ("Bipartisan Infrastructure Law"), Amendment No. 1*, G4910-9X, January 3, 2023.

Office of the Under Secretary for Policy, U.S. Department of Transportation, *How to Compete for FY 2022 RAISE Transportation Discretionary Grants*, briefing slides, c. February 2022.

OMB Circular A-4—*See* Office of Management and Budget, 2003.

OMB Circular A-11—*See* Office of Management and Budget, 2016.

OMB Circular A-19—*See* Office of Management and Budget, 1979.

OMB Circular A-87—*See* Office of Management and Budget, 2004.

OMB Circular A-94—*See* Office of Management and Budget, 1992.

Panel on Methods and Techniques of Project Analysis, Committee to Assess the U.S. Army Corps of Engineers Methods of Analysis and Peer Review for Water Resources Project Planning, Water Science and Technology Board, Ocean Studies Board, Division on Earth and Life Studies, National Academy of Sciences, *Analytical Methods and Approaches for Water Resources Project Planning*, National Academies Press, 2004.

Parker, Brittney, and Jessie Ritter, *Building Resilience Through Natural Infrastructure: Barriers and Opportunities Within FEMA Hazard Mitigation and HUD Community Development Block Grant Programs*, prepared for Theodore Roosevelt Conservation Partnership and the Water Foundation, July 23, 2021.

Pearce, David W., *Cost–Benefit Analysis*, Palgrave MacMillan, 2nd ed., October 20, 1983.

Perez v. Mortgage Bankers Association, 575 U.S. 92, March 9, 2015.

P&G—*See* Water Resources Council, 1983.

Planning and Environmental Division, Office of Airport Planning and Programming, Federal Aviation Administration, U.S. Department of Transportation, "Formulation of the National Plan of Integrated Airport Systems (NPIAS) and the Airports Capital Improvement Plan (ACIP)," Order 5090.5, September 3, 2019.

President's State, Local, and Tribal Leaders Task Force on Climate Preparedness and Resilience, *Recommendations to the President*, November 2014.

Public Law 67-13, Budget and Accounting Act, 1921, June 10, 1921.

Public Law 74-738, an act authorizing the construction of certain public works on rivers and harbors for flood control, and for other purposes, June 22, 1936.

Public Law 79-377, Federal Airport Act, May 13, 1946.

Public Law 79-404, Administrative Procedure Act, June 11, 1946.

Public Law 86-645, an act authorizing the construction, repair, and preservation of certain public works on rivers and harbors for navigation, flood control, and other purposes, July 14, 1960.

Public Law 89-80, Water Resources Planning Act, July 22, 1965.

Public Law 89-670, an act to establish a department of transportation, and for other purposes, October 15, 1966.

Public Law 91-190, National Environmental Policy Act of 1969, January 1, 1970.

Public Law 91-258, Airport and Airway Development Act of 1970, May 21, 1970.

Public Law 93-251, an act authorizing the construction, repair, and preservation of certain public works on rivers and harbors for navigation, flood control, and for other purposes, March 7, 1974.

Public Law 93-288, Disaster Relief Act Amendments of 1974, May 22, 1974.

Public Law 93-383, Housing and Community Development Act of 1974, August 22, 1974.

Public Law 97-248, Tax Equity and Fiscal Responsibility Act of 1982, September 3, 1982.

Public Law 97-276, joint resolution making continuing appropriations for the fiscal year 1983, and for other purposes, October 2, 1982.

Public Law 100-707, The Disaster Relief and Emergency Assistance Amendments of 1988, November 23, 1988.

Public Law 107-296, Homeland Security Act of 2002, November 25, 2002.

Public Law 108-7, Consolidated Appropriations Resolution, 2003, February 20, 2003.

Public Law 108-199, Consolidated Appropriations Act, 2004, January 23, 2004.

Public Law 108-447, Consolidated Appropriations Act, 2005, December 8, 2004.

Public Law 110-114, Water Resources Development Act of 2007, November 8, 2007.

Public Law 110-161, Consolidated Appropriations Act, 2008, December 26, 2007.

Public Law 111-5, American Recovery and Reinvestment Act of 2009, February 17, 2009.

Public Law 111-117, Consolidated Appropriations Act, 2010, December 16, 2009.

Public Law 112-25, Budget Control Act of 2011, August 2, 2011.

Public Law 112-74, Consolidated Appropriations Act, 2012, December 23, 2011.

Public Law 115-254, FAA Reauthorization Act of 2018, October 5, 2018.

Public Law 116-260, Consolidated Appropriations Act, 2021, December 27, 2020.

Public Law 117-58, Infrastructure Investment and Jobs Act, November 15, 2021.

Public Law 117-103, Consolidated Appropriations Act, 2022, March 15, 2022.

Risk Reduction Division, Federal Insurance and Mitigation Administration, Federal Emergency Management Agency, U.S. Department of Homeland Security, "Strategic Funds Management Implementation Guide for the Hazard Mitigation Grant Program," job aid, February 24, 2015.

Roman-Romero, Jorge, "The Hispanic/Latino Case Against Kaldor–Hicks Cost–Benefit Analysis in Risk Regulation," *Harvard Kennedy School Journal of Hispanic Policy*, Vol. 34, Spring 2022.

Scitovsky, Tibor, "Inequalities: Open and Hidden, Measured and Immeasurable," *Annals of the American Academy of Political and Social Science*, Vol. 409, September 1973.

Seelye, Katharine Q., and John Tierney, "E.P.A. Drops Age-Based Cost Studies," *New York Times*, May 8, 2003.

Skidmore v. Swift and Co., 323 U.S. 134, December 9, 1944.

Spielman, Seth E., Joseph Tuccillo, David C. Folch, Amy Schweikert, Rebecca Davies, Nathan Wood, and Eric Tate, "Evaluating Social Vulnerability Indicators: Criteria and Their Application to the Social Vulnerability Index," *Natural Hazards*, Vol. 100, January 2020.

Stafford Act—*See* Public Law 93-288, 1974, and 42 U.S.C. Chapter 68.

Sunstein, Cass R., "Valuing Life: A Plea for Disaggregation," *Duke Law Journal*, Vol. 54, 2004.

Tang, Rachel Y., *Financing Airport Improvements*, Congressional Research Service, updated March 15, 2019.

United States v. Mead Corp., 533 U.S. 218, 2001.

USACE—*See* U.S. Army Corps of Engineers.

U.S. Army Corps of Engineers, Department of the Army, *Planning Guidance Notebook*, Engineer Regulation 1105-2-100, April 22, 2000.

U.S. Army Corps of Engineers, Department of the Army, *Principles and Requirements for Federal Investments in Water Resources*, March 2013.

U.S. Army Corps of Engineers, "Incorporating Life Safety into Flood and Costal [sic] Storm Risk Management Studies," Planning Bulletin 2019-04, June 20, 2019.

U.S. Code, Title 2, Grants and Agreements.

U.S. Code, Title 5, Government Organization and Employees.

U.S. Code, Title 6, Domestic Security; Chapter 1, Homeland Security Organization; Subchapter III, Science and Technology in Support of Homeland Security; Section 185, Federally Funded Research and Development Centers.

U.S. Code, Title 23, Highways; Chapter 1, Federal-Aid Highways; Section 117, Nationally Significant Multimodal Freight and Highway Projects.

U.S. Code, Title 31, Money and Finance; Subtitle II, The Budget Process; Chapter 11, The Budget and Fiscal, Budget, and Program Information; Section 1111, Improving Economy and Efficiency.

U.S. Code, Title 42, The Public Health and Welfare.

U.S. Code, Title 44, Part 78, Flood Mitigation Assistance.

U.S. Code, Title 44, Part 79, Flood Mitigation Grants.

U.S. Department of Housing and Urban Development, "CDBG-MIT Overview," webpage, undated-a. As of July 11, 2022:
https://www.hudexchange.info/programs/cdbg-mit/overview/

U.S. Department of Housing and Urban Development, "HUD Exchange," homepage, undated-b. As of July 11, 2022:
https://www.hudexchange.info/

U.S. Department of Housing and Urban Development, *Appendix H: Phase 2 Benefit–Cost Analysis (BCA) Instructions for Community Development Block Grant National Disaster Resilience (CDBG-NDR) Applicants*, June 2015.

U.S. Department of Housing and Urban Development, "Community Development Block Grant Program," webpage, content current as of June 2, 2022. As of July 11, 2022:
https://www.hud.gov/program_offices/comm_planning/cdbg

U.S. Department of Transportation, "Transportation Disadvantaged Census Tracts (Historically Disadvantaged Communities)," webpage, undated. As of July 18, 2022:
https://usdot.maps.arcgis.com/apps/dashboards/d6f90dfcc8b44525b04c7ce748a3674a

U.S. Department of Transportation, "Treatment of the Value of Preventing Fatalities and Injuries in Preparing Economic Analyses," departmental guidance, March 2021a.

U.S. Department of Transportation, "FY 2023 RAISE Webinar Series," webpage, updated April 29, 2021b. As of July 19, 2022:
https://www.transportation.gov/RAISEgrants/outreach

U.S. Government Accountability Office, *Intercity Passenger and Freight Rail: Better Data and Communication of Uncertainties Can Help Decision Makers Understand Benefits and Trade-Offs of Programs and Policies*, GAO-11-290, February 24, 2011.

U.S. Government Accountability Office, *U.S. Army Corps of Engineers: Information on Evaluations of Benefits and Costs for Water Resources Development Projects and OMB's Review*, GAO-20-113-R, December 18, 2019.

U.S. Government Accountability Office, *Disaster Resilience: FEMA Should Take Additional Steps to Streamline Hazard Mitigation Grants and Assess Program Effects*, GAO-21-140, February 2, 2021.

U.S. Senate, *Policies, Standards, and Procedures in the Formulation, Evaluation, and Review of Plans for Use and Development of Water and Related Land Resources*, 87th Congress, 2nd Session, May 29, 1962.

Water Resources Council, "Water and Related Land Resources: Establishment of Principles and Standards for Planning," *Federal Register*, Vol. 38, No. 174, September 10, 1973.

Water Resources Council, *Economic and Environmental Principles for Water and Related Land Resources Implementation Studies*, March 10, 1983.

Weitzman, Martin L., "Why the Far-Distant Future Should Be Discounted at Its Lowest Possible Rate," *Journal of Environmental Economics and Management*, Vol. 36, 1998.

White House, "Fact Sheet: President Biden's Executive Actions on Climate to Address Extreme Heat and Boost Offshore Wind," press release, July 20, 2022.

Young, Shalanda D., acting director, Office of Management and Budget; Brenda Mallory, chair, Council on Environmental Quality; and Gina McCarthy, national climate adviser, "Interim Implementation Guidance for the Justice40 Initiative," memorandum M-21-28, July 20, 2021.